SERVING THE LORD: THE BOOK OF JAMES

A Bible Study on Putting Your Faith into Practice

MARCI OGROSKY

WESTBOW
PRESS®
A DIVISION OF THOMAS NELSON
& ZONDERVAN

Scripture quotations are from The Holy Bible, English Standard Version® (ESV®), copyright © 2001 by Crossway, a publishing ministry of Good News Publishers. Used by permission. All rights reserved.

WestBow Press books may be ordered through booksellers or by contacting:

WestBow Press
A Division of Thomas Nelson & Zondervan
1663 Liberty Drive
Bloomington, IN 47403
www.westbowpress.com
1 (866) 928-1240

ISBN: 978-1-5127-1789-1 (sc)
ISBN: 978-1-5127-1788-4 (e)

Library of Congress Control Number: 2015917960

Print information available on the last page.

WestBow Press rev. date: 11/11/2015

Contents

THE *Faith* TRILOGY

A series of three Bible study guides by Marci Ogrosky designed to explore
your faith from three different perspectives: head, heart and hands

Also available in the series:

Looking to Christ: The Book of Hebrews
A Bible study on keeping the faith when you are discouraged

God's Cranky Prophets: Jonah & Habakkuk
A Bible study on responding in faith when you don't like what God is doing

⮞ Time Line ⮜

B.C. (Before Christ)
or B.C.E. (Before the Common Era)

Adam & Eve (Creation)

Noah (Flood)

2000	Abraham (Patriarchs)
1500	Moses (Exodus)
1000	David (United Kingdom)
500	Return from Exile

A.D. *(Anno Domini,*
In the Year of Our Lord)
or C.E. (the Common Era)

1	JESUS CHRIST James
500	Mohammed (Islam, 600s)
1000	Catholic/Orthodox Split
1500	Luther, Calvin (Reformation)
2000	Us

❧ Introduction ❧

One thing people like about the book of James is its practical approach to Christian commitment. The book answers the question, *What does it look like to be a servant of the Lord, especially when facing trials of various kinds?* Here is down-to-earth application of doctrinal truth that will benefit every believer no matter where they are on their faith journey.

The author identifies himself as James, a servant of God and the Lord Jesus Christ. This is probably Jesus' younger brother James. He is initially portrayed in Scripture as opposing Jesus' ministry but by grace became a believer, a leader of the church, and finally a martyr. His self-identity as a willing servant is the same identity all Christians should embrace out of gratitude for salvation in Christ.

Serving the Lord involves loyalty, moral living, mercy toward others, and perseverance. We are to strive for spiritual maturity and be fruitful in producing good works, not to earn salvation but to give evidence of our faith now and at the end times. James encourages us to put our faith into practice even in the face of trials, for trials can serve a redemptive purpose:

> "Count it all joy, my brothers, when you meet trials of various kinds,
> for you know that the testing of your faith produces steadfastness.
> And let steadfastness have its full effect, that you may be
> perfect and complete, lacking in nothing."
> (James 1:2-4)

Ancient church historians confirm James' reputation as a righteous and pious man. Hegesippus (2nd century) writes that James was obedient to his life-long Nazirite vow. He developed knees as hard as a camel's due to long hours in prayer for God's people and was nicknamed "James the Just" by the apostles due to his passion for honoring God's law and righteousness.[1] Eusebius (4th century) says James was chosen by the apostles to be the first bishop or overseer of the Jerusalem mother church.[2]

James assumes his readers already know and accept the basic beliefs of the Christian faith. He builds on underlying theological truths such as:

Jesus Christ is our Lord and Savior, God Himself.
People were created by God to glorify Him in word and deed.
Salvation from sin is by grace alone, through Christ's work alone.
Believers are part of the body of Christ, the church.
There will be final judgment when Christ returns at the end times.

The book of James is reminiscent of the Old Testament book of Proverbs and often echoes Jesus' teachings, particularly the Sermon on the Mount. Both Jesus and James promote the correct practice of faith (orthopraxy), teaching that faith and works are a unity that cannot be separated:

"And everyone who hears these words of mine and does not do them
will be like a foolish man who built his house on the sand."
(Matthew 7:26)

"But be doers of the word, and not hearers only, deceiving yourselves."
(James 1:22)

James agrees with Jesus that good intentions are not enough. Neglecting to perform deeds of mercy is as serious an offense to Christ as committing sinful acts. Both Jesus and James condemn the failure to put faith into practice:

"For I was hungry and you gave me no food, I was thirsty and you
gave me no drink, I was a stranger and you did not welcome
me, naked and you did not clothe me... as you did not do it
to one of the least of these, you did not do it to me."
(Matthew 25:42-45)

"If a brother or sister is poorly clothed and lacking in daily food, and
one of you says to them, 'Go in peace, be warmed and filled,' without

giving them the things needed for the body, what good is that?
So also faith by itself, if it does not have works, is dead."
(James 2:15-17)

This study guide is designed for group or individual Bible study. The lessons provide background information, related Scripture references, and study questions to deepen the reader's understanding of the Bible passage along with its application to our lives. There are six sets of study questions per lesson, making it easier to study the lesson a little at a time during a week. A leader's guide and other appendices are provided near the end of the book.

The closing devotion for each lesson comes from Andrew Murray's short book, *Working for God!*, in which he encourages all Christians to be doers of the word, not hearers only. Murray was a well-loved and respected 19th century pastor in South Africa. His devotional writings have inspired countless Christians around the world.

It is hoped that your study of the book of James will motivate you to persevere joyfully through the trials of life as a devoted servant of God and the Lord Jesus Christ. May you serve the Lord well by putting your faith into practice in all kinds of circumstances so as to produce the fruit of good works for the glory of God.

SERVING THE LORD: THE BOOK OF JAMES

A Bible Study on Putting Your Faith into Practice

❧ *Lesson 1* ❧
Persevering With Joy

James 1:1-18

Welcome to this study of the New Testament book of James. Before you start this lesson, please take time to read all five chapters of the book of James in your Bible to get an overview. As you read, continually ask yourself what it looks like in practical terms to be a servant of God and Jesus Christ.

Part I: Setting the Stage

Purpose
This lesson introduces us to the author James and his startling command to consider it all joy when we face trials of various kinds. Trials are meant to mature our faith and develop spiritual endurance so we will persevere in faith to the end of life. It is important for us to realize that God uses trials for the good of His devoted servants, and therefore trials have a redemptive purpose for Christians.

Look for the following application points in this lesson:

1. Christians are to serve Jesus Christ with the heart of a devoted servant.
2. We should ask God for wisdom to deal with trials.
3. We should consider it all joy when we face trials because trials serve a redemptive purpose for Christians.

Author

The opening verse names the author simply as James. The identity of this James was a matter of dispute in certain parts of the early church.[3] The most prominent James was the apostle James, brother of John, but he was martyred before the book was written. Scholars now widely agree that the author is the esteemed James the Just, the younger half-brother of Jesus.

Date

The Lord's brother James took over leadership of the Jerusalem church after Herod executed the apostle James in A.D. 44 and arrested the apostle Peter. The book of James may have been written as early as 47, for it does not mention issues discussed at the Jerusalem Council moderated by James in 49. James' letter is possibly the earliest writing in the New Testament, followed by Paul's letter to the Galatians around 49-50.

Audience

The book of James is a letter (epistle) written for general distribution to Jewish Christians dispersed or scattered outside Palestine. This dispersion *(diaspora)* was brought about by persecution from Jewish authorities starting with the martyrdom of Stephen, a leader in the Jerusalem church. Persecuted believers fled to Phoenicia, Cyprus, Antioch Syria, and further.

Themes

Several significant themes are interwoven and repeated throughout the letter, such as the following:

- God's righteousness, holiness, grace, and wisdom
- Jesus Christ's royal law of love
- Perseverance in suffering and trials
- Humble obedience and reliance on God
- The unity of faith and works
- Holy and moral living, including control of the tongue
- Final judgment and glory

Outline

It is not easy to categorize the material in the book of James by chapters. Sometimes James discusses various topics within a chapter or revisits a theme in several different chapters. The loose structure allows scholars to outline the material in a variety of valid ways. The following is a simple outline featuring important aspects of being a servant of the Lord:

Chapter 1   Perseverance in trials
Chapter 2   Faith and good works
Chapter 3   Heavenly wisdom
Chapter 4   Moral living
Chapter 5   Reliance on God

Part II: Studying Scripture

1.   James the Lord's Brother

a)   Read Mark 3:20-21, 31-35; and 6:3-6. Jesus and James were half-brothers born to the same mother Mary.[4] How did the family react when Jesus began to attract crowds? How did Jesus react to His family? What does this tell you about James' spiritual condition at this point in Jesus' ministry?

b)   Read Luke 14:26. In what sense do you think Jesus meant His followers must "hate" or love less their earthly ties to family and life? What should His followers put first? What does this priority look like in your life?

c)   Read John 7:1-10. Jesus' brothers urged Him to go to Jerusalem despite the potential danger, presumably to preach openly to prove He was the Messiah. Why do unbelievers then and now demand that Jesus prove Himself beyond the miracles He performed? Why is there really no proof unbelievers will accept?

Read James 1:1

2. James the Lord's Servant

We do not know when James became a believer, but scholars usually identify the defining moment as Jesus' resurrection appearance. By grace James was changed forever from unbeliever to believer, pill to pillar, mocker to martyr, from thinking Jesus was insane to knowing He is the truth.

a) In v. 1, James calls himself a servant of God and Jesus Christ. His servant identity has a dual connotation. First, it evokes the authority of Old Testament prophets chosen by God to be His spokespersons.[5] Second, it conveys submission, for James uses the word for a voluntary bondservant (*doulos*) who is paying off a debt. What does it mean to be this kind of servant? What does this tell you about the way James sees himself? Do you see yourself this way in relation to Christ?

b) James refers to Jesus as Lord and Christ. The title Christ is the Greek translation of the Hebrew title Messiah, emphasizing the saving work of Jesus. What do the references to lordship and salvation tell you about the way James sees Jesus? How will you learn to see Jesus this way more fully?

c) Why is it a mark of humility that James does not call himself Jesus' brother?

d) The resurrected Jesus appeared individually to Peter, James, and Paul (I Corinthians 15:3-8), all of whom would become central figures in the early church. Read Acts 1:14. After Jesus ascended to heaven, His followers waited in the Upper Room until Jesus sent His Holy Spirit to empower them. What phrases confirm that James was now a believer aligned with the apostles?

e) Read Galatians 1:18-19; 2:9; and Acts 21:17-19. Paul consulted with James at the beginning and end of his ministry. What does Paul acknowledge about James in Galatians 2:9a? What does this tell you about James' stature among the apostles?

Read James 1:2-12

3. Facing Trials with Faith and Joy

The road from faith and trials to the soul's perfection upon death is the normal Christian path. We can also think of trials and perfection as links in a chain:

The Chain of Faith
Faith + Trials → Testing → Steadfastness → Perfection (Eternal Life)

a) "Count it all joy" (*charan*) continues the thought behind the previous word "Greetings" (*chairein*, literally "joy"). It is as if James is saying "Joy, count it all joy!" How are you doing at responding to troubles in this counter-intuitive way? What types of troubles are difficult for you to count as joy? How will it be an encouragement to remember that trials can produce steadfastness?

b) In v. 2-4, James advises us to let trials become testing. The purpose is two-fold: to reveal the genuineness of our faith and develop our faith. Why do the difficulties of life tend to provide more opportunity for testing and spiritual growth than calm times? How has your own experience verified this?

c) How is the Chain of Faith expressed in the passages below?

Romans 5:3-4	Faith + Suffering →	_____
I Peter 1:6-7	Faith + Trials →	_____
Revelation 2:10	Faith + Suffering →	_____

d) Read Romans 8:28. Describe a difficult time that caused you anxiety, but you later realized that God brought something good out of it. What did that experience teach you about responding to trials with faith and joy?

e) When a trial comes, we often do not respond with joy because we do not know how to handle the problem. What assurance does James give to believers in v. 5? How will this assurance affect the way you deal with troubles?

f) In v. 6-8, a doubter is like a wave of the sea, a symbol of chaos in Scripture. James is not talking about someone who asks honest questions, but someone who waivers between heavenly and worldly wisdom, ultimately judging God's wisdom to be wrong. The doubter is double-minded (*dipsychos,* literally "two-souled"), a term coined by James to describe divided loyalty. Why do we need to have single-minded loyalty to God in order to benefit from His wisdom?

4. Facing Trials with Perseverance

a) In v. 9, the readers in general are apparently impoverished, perhaps due to persecution. Read Luke 1:52. How does James echo Jesus' teaching about the status of the poor in God's kingdom?

b) Read Jeremiah 9:23-24. What should people boast about?

c) In v. 10-11, James quotes the prophet Isaiah's warning that we are mere mortals whose earthly glory will not last. Read Isaiah 40:6-8. What is lasting?

d) In v. 12, the Chain of Faith culminates in a victor's crown (*stephanos*), a wreath of leaves awarded to the winner of an athletic event. The crown of life could be a reference to finishing earthly life or to eternal life in heaven. Read Matthew 5:10-12. How does James echo Jesus' teaching in the Beatitudes?

Read James 1:13-18

5. Facing Trials with Unbelief

Responding to trials with faith can turn trials into tests that strengthen our faith. Responding to trials with unbelieving evil desires, though, can turn trials into temptations to sin. The chain of unbelief leads to death:

The Chain of Unbelief
Evil Desires + Trials → Temptation → Sin → Death (Eternal Death)

a) One definition of temptation is being enticed to get what one wants by doing something wrong. It is not a sin to be tempted, but it is a sin to give in to temptation. In v. 13, why can we never blame God for our temptations? In other words, what do we know about God's character and actions?

b) In v. 14, James uses fishing imagery to describe how our evil desires compel us toward temptation. Our desires "lure" us (meaning they drag or carry us away forcefully) and "entice" us (meaning they attract us, as if toward bait). What practical suggestions do you have for resisting temptation?

c) Read I Corinthians 10:13 and 6:18. God always provides a way out of temptation, but we must do the resisting and fleeing. With regard to sexual temptation, although Scripture assures us there is no temptation too great to resist, why do you suppose it is best to flee rather than stay around to fight it?

d) In v. 15, James uses childbearing imagery to show the natural progression of sin. What is the result of giving in to evil desires?

6. God's Redemptive Purposes

a) In v. 16, what lies or self-deception is James warning us about? Be sure to look back at v. 13-15 and forward to v. 17 to get the complete picture.

b) In v. 17, the title "Father of lights" is not found elsewhere in Scripture. It may refer to God's role as the Creator who made the sun, moon, stars, and planets. Name some changes that occur with these heavenly lights. How will it help you to face trials knowing that God's character, promises, and purposes, unlike created things, are unchanging? (Numbers 23:19; Psalm 102:25-27)

c) In v. 18, James uses childbearing imagery positively. God brought us forth (literally, "gave birth to us") so we might have faith. This good gift of spiritual regeneration is an act of grace. We are the firstfruits of God's creatures, meaning the most important and the first to be restored in God's redemptive plan. How does the knowledge of your high significance increase your desire to please God?

d) Pastor George Stulac summarizes the message of James:

> "This is the theme of his letter: How shall we live as servants of the Lord Jesus Christ?... His burden in writing is this: 'Don't put off your life of faith until times get better.

Right now, in the midst of your suffering, is the time to be putting your servanthood toward Christ into practice.'

"The message is clearly applicable for Christians today... Now is the very time to practice the joy, peace and love that we know theoretically to be the Christian life. For the Christian life is not mere theory; it is the life of the servant of God and the Lord Jesus Christ."[6]

Part III: Personal Application and Growth

Today's lesson points to several important truths that apply to our personal lives. Allow these truths to penetrate your mind, soften your heart, deepen your faith and affect your behavior to help you continually grow in Christ.

1. Christians are to serve Jesus Christ with the heart of a devoted servant.

How will you live as a loyal servant of Christ, putting Jesus ahead of earthly ties to family and friends while still honoring your commitments to them?

2. We should ask God for wisdom to deal with trials.

Take your anxieties to God in prayer today with confidence that He will give you His wisdom. What practical difference do you expect to see in your life as you replace anxiety with assurance that God will answer in His good time?

3. We should consider it all joy when we face trials because trials serve a redemptive purpose for Christians.

Instead of responding to trials with worry, anxiety, evil desires, withdrawal, denial, self-pity, complaining, or selfishness, what steps will you take to respond to trials with faith and joy? What will you do to see each trial as a tool God can use to strengthen your faith muscles to help you persevere in faith?

Part IV: Closing Devotion
by Andrew Murray

It requires a living faith to take pleasure in our weaknesses, and in weakness to do our work, knowing that God is working in us. Without seeing or feeling anything, to go on in the confidence of a hidden power working in us – this is the highest exercise of a life of faith.

Persevering in prayer and labor amid outwardly unfavorable circumstances and appearances, still to labor more abundantly – faith alone can do this. Let us be strong in faith, giving glory to God.

Christian! Be willing to yield yourself to the very utmost to God, that His power may rest upon you, may work in you. Offer yourself to Him for His work as the one object of your life. Count upon His working all in you, to fit you for His service, to strengthen and bless you in it.

Let the faith and love of your Lord Jesus, whose strength is going to be made perfect in your weakness, lead you to live even as He did, to do the Father's will.[7]

Lesson 2
Obeying God's Word

James 1:19-27

Part I: Setting the Stage

Purpose

This lesson examines the importance of obeying God in thought, word, and deed as His faithful servants. We are to respond to God's word with holy living and practical good works.

Look for the following application points in this lesson:

1. Christians should be advised by God's saving word.
2. We are to control our anger and speech.
3. Pure religion is demonstrated by holy living and deeds of mercy.

The Perfect Law

James has a passion for obeying God's word revealed in the Old Testament Mosaic Law, called the perfect law, but he writes with a thoroughly Christian understanding. To better appreciate what James is saying about the need for us to obey the law, let us take a closer look at it.

The Mosaic Law (Law of Moses) is recorded in the Torah, the first five books of the Old Testament (Genesis through Deuteronomy). The 613 laws and commands found in the Torah can be organized into three basic categories. We should not think of these categories as distinct from one another, though, since some laws fit into more than one category and religion was not separated from the government and social life of ancient Israel:

- Civil Law: These laws governed judicial, political, and social aspects of the theocracy of ancient Israel, which came to an end in A.D. 70. Israel's civil law was fulfilled in Christ, the ultimate King.
- Ceremonial Law: These laws regulated Levitical worship and ritual sacrifices in ancient Israel. The ceremonial law was fulfilled in Christ, the ultimate High Priest.
- Moral Law: These laws apply to all people throughout the ages and are still applicable today. They are summarized in the Ten Commandments. Christ is the fulfillment and embodiment of the moral law.[8]

The Mosaic Law, also called the old covenant, was a good thing and could even be called perfect or complete in its time, but it was limited in some significant ways. For instance, the old covenant's ceremonial sacrificial system could not cleanse a sinner's guilty conscience fully or permanently, nor empower a sinner to obey God's word.

The Law of Liberty

Jesus Christ mediated a new covenant that accomplished what the old covenant of Mosaic Law could not. In Christ the sinner's guilty conscience is cleansed once for all, and the indwelling Holy Spirit enables the believer to obey God's word (Hebrews 8:6-13; 9:13-14; Romans 8:2). Because Jesus Christ fulfilled the perfect law (Matthew 5:17), we are now under what James calls the law of liberty, the gospel.

The gospel brings us liberty in several ways. We are free from the burden of trying to earn salvation since Christ accomplished perfect obedience to the law in our place (Galatians 5:1-4). We are also free from the power of sin and death and from the consequences of God's wrath due to our sin.

Life in Christ

The grace of the gospel infiltrates all of James' teaching. He is not interested in legalistic obedience to God's commandments and rules so we will lead a respectable life. Rather, James insists that living a righteous life is the outgrowth of our relationship with Christ. Christians obey God's word because they want to serve and please their loving Lord and Savior. They make a moral commitment to Him out of gratitude for who He is and what He has done.

Living out our faith involves deeds of mercy and holy living. While it is true that faith has an intellectual and theoretical aspect, it is made complete only when we demonstrate it in practical ways that produce good fruit:

> "Religion that is pure and undefiled before God, the Father,
> is this: to visit orphans and widows in their affliction, and
> to keep oneself unstained from the world." (James 1:27)

Part II: Studying Scripture

Read James 1:19-21

God's saving grace is the context for this passage and the entire letter. It is the reason why believers should urgently and unconditionally obey God's word.

1. Be Advised by God's Word

a) Take a moment to think about seeking good advice. To whom in your life do you turn for wisdom? Why do you listen to that person?

b) In v. 19, how does James address the readers? Note that sisters in Christ are included. What is James trying to convey to the readers and what effect would it have on them?

c) What should believers be quick to do? Slow to do? Although this is good advice in general, James is not giving a lesson on manners. Rather, he urges us not to speak carelessly from our own sinful desires. We are to be eager to listen to God's implanted word, the gospel, and let our attitudes, words, and actions be advised by it.

d) Speech and anger are paired together here because there is a connection between words and feelings. In general, unguarded words express one's inner feelings and desires. Words that are hurtful, untrue, selfish, or angry reveal sinful inner desires. Why does listening to God's implanted word, meaning the gospel, make us slow to anger?

e) In v. 20, why is it spiritually harmful for us to live in anger? Although there is such a thing as righteous anger such as Jesus exhibited at times, much of our anger is demanding and self-interested. Why does selfish anger indicate we are not listening to God? How will you ensure that you listen to God better?

2. Discard the Sinful Life

a) In v. 21a, James uses clothing imagery. The phrase "put away all filthiness" refers to taking off dirty clothes and is used in the New Testament to mean getting rid of sinful, pre-Christian behavior. What word describes the extent of wickedness or evil in the unbeliever's life (translations will vary)?

b) God renews the hearts of believers so they are able to respond to His word. Why do you think it is more difficult for believers to rightly respond to God's word if they continue to be involved in the old sinful way of life?

c) How would you use the clothing image to explain to someone young in the faith that God expects believers to replace their sinful way of life with a new way of life in Christ?

3. Nurture God's Word

a) In v. 21b, James uses gardening imagery when he says God implants His word, the gospel, in believers. God's word needs to be accepted and cared for. After conversion we must continue to nurture the word for the rest of our lives. Name some ways you can nurture God's word in your heart so it continues to grow in you with the help of the Holy Spirit.

b) We are to receive the gospel in meekness or humility, not in arrogant pride. Why does our humble reliance on God increase our ability to benefit from God's word?

c) According to James, what is the result of accepting the implanted word, the gospel of Christ?

Read James 1:22-25

4. Obey God's Word

a) In v. 22, what have we done to ourselves when we hear God's word but do not act on it?

b) In v. 23-24, James illustrates his point by comparing God's word to a mirror. When people study their face in a mirror, it reflects what they are like. If they deceive themselves into thinking there is nothing they need to do or they fail to make improvements, they get no lasting benefit from the mirror. It is useless to them. How is this similar to hearing God's word and not acting on it?

c) Why are we so often willing to read Scripture and walk away from it without applying it in practical ways? What will you do to ensure that your study of the Bible leads to tangible applications in your life?

d) In v. 25, what does James say about someone who hears God's word and perseveres in acting on it?

e) Read Luke 11:27-28. How does James' teaching echo what Jesus taught?

5. Appreciate God's Word

a) In v. 25, God's word is called the "perfect" law, a reference to the Mosaic Law of the Old Testament. Read Psalm 19:7-8 and list four ways God's people were to benefit from the Law. Describe a time when you felt the kind of appreciation for God's word that the psalmist displays.

b) God's word is also called the law of "liberty," a likely reference to Jesus' teachings and fulfillment of the Law. The law of liberty can be equated with the gospel, the "word of truth" that brings regeneration (v. 18), and the "implanted word" that leads to salvation (v. 21). It frees us from trying to earn our salvation and frees us from the power of sin. How will you express gratitude to God for this freedom?

c) True blessing lies in a life of active obedience to God's word. Why do you think anyone would be willing to miss out on God's blessings by failing to appreciate or live in accordance with His word?

Read James 1:26-27

6. Apply God's Word

a) Taming the tongue is an important theme in the book of James. In v. 26, why would unbridled or uncontrolled speech be incompatible with being godly or religious?

b) Mercy ministry is another major theme in the book of James. In v. 27, what does James exhort believers to do? Give an example of what it means to visit the defenseless in their distress.

c) Read Exodus 22:21-24. The orphan, widow, and foreigner living among God's people symbolize the poor and oppressed people of the world. Why can there be no doubt that God has a heart for the needy? Note the poetic justice of the punishment for those who would mistreat and allow the poor to die.

d) Read Isaiah 1:23. In the time of the prophet Isaiah, why were Israel's leaders failing to care for the poor and how had the justice system failed?

e) In what ways do similar problems exist in our society today? List some reasons Christians today do not get more involved in insisting on justice for the poor and needy. How can we do better?

f) Words that articulate the gospel message are to be accompanied by deeds of mercy that authenticate the message. Would you say you tend to favor action or words in your outreach efforts? What will you do to include both aspects? Pastor Chris Sicks points out the necessity of ministering in word and deed:

> "God's people need to proclaim the gospel, and also work hard to provide tangible evidence that this grace is true – that God actually cares... Don't assume that people understand the connection between your Christian faith and the mercy you offer. Be sure to tell them about the Source of your love and how they can know Him."[9]

g) Holy living is another prominent theme in the book of James. This involves more than ethical conduct; James is talking about behavior that is motivated by and grounded in a personal relationship with God. In v. 27, what does the image of stains or pollution tell you about the difficulty of removing the influence of worldliness from our lives? Give some examples of the kinds of worldly influences that stain or pollute (literally, "blemish") us.

Part III: Personal Application and Growth

Today's lesson points to several important truths that apply to our personal lives. Allow these truths to penetrate your mind, soften your heart, deepen your faith and affect your behavior to help you continually grow in Christ.

1. Christians should be advised by God's saving word.

Think of an area in your life where you tend to follow worldly wisdom rather than God's word. What steps will you take to be informed about God's word in that area and try to obey it? What changes in your life do you expect to see as you follow more closely what God says in Scripture?

2. We are to control our anger and speech.

The next time you hear yourself speaking in self-righteous anger, what will you do to stop and listen to God's implanted word? How will you know if you are ready to speak rightly? Ask a close friend to hold you accountable for controlling your angry words.

3. Pure religion is demonstrated by holy living and deeds of mercy.

What will you do this week to make a positive difference in the life of the defenseless? How will you allow deeds of mercy to become your habit?

Part IV: Closing Devotion
by Andrew Murray

In nothing is the power of sin more clearly seen than this, that even in the believer there is such a gap between intellect and conduct. It is possible to delight in hearing, to be diligent in increasing our knowledge of God's word, to admire and approve the truth, even to be willing to do it, and yet to fail entirely in the actual performance. Hence the warning of James.

We are ever inclined to seek our blessedness in what God gives, in privilege and enjoyment. But Christ placed it in what we *do*, because it is only in doing that we really prove and know and possess the life God has bestowed. Doing is the very essence of blessedness, the highest manifestation, and therefore the fullest enjoyment of the life of God.

Only begin. Pray for and depend on the promised grace. Give yourself to a ministry of love; in the very nature of things, in the example of Christ, in the promise of God you have the assurance: Blessed is the doer![10]

❧ *Lesson 3* ❧

Showing Mercy

James 2:1-13

Part I: Setting the Stage

Purpose

This lesson takes a closer look at what it means to be merciful, a vital aspect of serving the Lord. Christians are especially called to show compassion to the poor and defenseless. Mercy should triumph over judgment. It is important to remember that Christians are to be merciful, for God has shown mercy to them in Christ.

Look for the following application points in this lesson:

1. Christians must not show favoritism based on external appearances.
2. Jesus calls us not to judge wrongly, but to judge rightly.
3. We are to show mercy to others because God shows it to us.

God's Goodness

One of the ways theologians describe God is to say He is personal rather than impersonal. By this they mean that God is person-like. He is a Being with characteristics and attributes, much the same way that humans have attributes. Some of God's attributes are shared with humans to a certain extent, such as love and goodness, while other attributes belong to God alone, such as omniscience and omnipotence.

God's attribute of goodness is expressed through His mercy, grace, and patience. Scripture does not always make a clear distinction between these traits and sometimes mercy and grace in particular seem to be used synonymously. The following definitions acknowledge the active nature of God's goodness expressed in grace and mercy:

- Grace (*hanan* in Hebrew; *charis* in Greek): God's unmerited favor shown to sinners. It contains the idea of forgiveness, strength, and provision of what is needed.
- Mercy (*hesed* or *racham* in Hebrew; *eleos* in Greek): God's undeserved goodness shown to those in misery or distress. It carries the meaning of lovingkindness, tender compassion, pity, and pardon.

Mercy Triumphs Over Judgment

Just as God has shown mercy to us in our sinfulness, we are to show mercy to others. When we fail to show mercy it indicates that our hearts are hard and unable to receive mercy from God. A hard heart will not benefit from God's saving work in Christ.

When God regenerates and softens our hearts, we must not continue to live in the old, hard way. For example, we must fight the temptation to judge others on the basis of external appearances such as expensive or shabby clothing. We should learn to look at people through God's perspective of compassion and love so we are able to respond to them with right discernment as He would.

The Royal Law of Love

When James talks about keeping unpolluted by the world, his discussion is rooted firmly in God's word, the law. In the previous lesson he dealt with both the perfect law, a reference to the Mosaic Law which was fulfilled in Jesus Christ, and the law of liberty, meaning the gospel and teachings of Christ. Now James speaks about something he calls the royal law.

Some commentators think the royal law is the same thing as the command to love your neighbor, while others equate it with the Mosaic Law which finds true moral expression in love for your neighbor. Still others are probably right to broaden the definition of the royal law to include not only Old Testament Scripture but also the gospel and teachings of Jesus, thus equating the royal law with all of God's supreme and loving word.

We are to bring everything in our hearts, speech, behavior, and relationships under the authority of God's word and we are to conduct our whole lives by His royal law of love. This can only be accomplished by complete reliance on God's grace. The result will be peace, the growth of our spiritual maturity, and an increasing desire to honor the righteousness of God as His devoted servants.

Part II: Studying Scripture

Read James 2:1-7

1. A Contrast in Glory

a) This is the only place in the letter besides the opening greeting where James refers to Jesus by name. The earthly name of Jesus together with His messianic titles Lord and Christ remind us He is both man and God. In v. 1, how else does James describe Jesus?

b) Try to imagine the incomparable radiance of Jesus, our risen Lord and Christ, our king and high priest who is enthroned forever at God's right hand. Describe the picture that comes to your mind when you contrast Jesus' surpassing glory and radiance with the splendor of the rich man in v. 2.

c) Why would James emphasize Jesus' glory at the beginning of a discussion about a rich man? How does the contrast between the glory of Jesus and that of the rich man put the rich man's status into proper perspective?

2. The Problem of External Appearances

a) In v. 2-3, James presents a hypothetical situation. He may have in mind a worship service or a meeting where converts are instructed.

The rich man and poor man are both described in terms of what they are wearing. Who is invited to have an honored seat? Who must either stand or sit on the floor, literally "under my footstool," in dishonor and humiliation?

b) James exhorts us to avoid showing partiality or favoritism based on external appearances. The Greek word for partiality means literally "receiving the face," meaning that a person is received on the basis of outward appearances. What are some external features besides expensive clothing and jewelry that might influence people to receive someone favorably today?

c) On the other hand, what are some external features that might cause people to treat someone with disfavor today?

d) The issue at stake is larger than how ushers should seat visitors at a church service. An underlying question is whether the poor will be fully welcomed into the life of the church. What do you think your church could be doing to better integrate low income worshipers into all aspects of church life?

e) In a church setting, favoritism toward the wealthy implies that having material riches is a factor in belonging to the kingdom of God. Explain in your own words why a Christian who shows favoritism is actually contradicting his or her faith in the sufficiency of Christ's work.

3. The Problem of Judging the Poor

a) In v. 4, what is wrong with showing partiality or favoritism?

b) What evil thoughts or selfish motives do you think would cause people to honor a rich person and dishonor the poor? What could people hope to gain by favoring the rich?

c) Read Matthew 7:1-5. Jesus forbids us to judge wrongly. Wrong judging is motivated by a selfish, fault-finding, condemning attitude that overlooks one's own failings. What happens when we judge with wrong motivations?

d) Read John 7:24. Jesus also commands us to judge rightly. Right judging involves a discerning, merciful attitude that honors God. What are two aspects of judging rightly according to the following verses?

I Samuel 16:7   _____

Luke 6:43-45   _____

e) Think of a time you mistakenly judged someone by external appearances but later discovered your judgment was wrong. What did you learn about your own prejudice? How will you avoid making the same mistake again?

f) Ministry leader Randy Nabors has a heart for the poor. He knows the humiliation of poverty and of being judged wrongly by others. He calls for us to participate in a ministry of mercy that helps the poor in a holistic way. What do you find compelling about his observations below?

"So yes, poverty is insulting. It insults you with the reminder today you don't have enough to eat, your clothes are inadequate... poverty mocks you with the disappointing realization there are places you can't go, events you can't experience, and things you can't have...

"Mercy as it pertains to the poor consists of two parts: charity and development... Charity (merciful relief) is the response of love to immediate human needs. Development is mercy extended to the poor in ways that empower them to help themselves, not only so they can become independent, but also to be merciful to others... Charity and development given without the Gospel or an articulation of the love of Christ is not a holistic or completed mercy."[11]

4. The Problem of Honoring the Wealthy

a) In v. 5, why would James address his readers with a term of endearment in the middle of his rebuke? Note that "brothers" includes sisters in Christ here.

b) Although the poor are not guaranteed salvation as a group, poor people tend to rely on God rather than their own resources. In v. 5, James offers good news to the poor. What is the unexpected fate of the poor who love God?

c) In v. 6-7, what is ironic about showing dishonor to the poor and honoring the wealthy? How do you suppose God feels about His people giving honor to the very people who dishonor His Son?

d) Christians bear the name of Christ, indicating they have a relationship with Him and are His representatives. The world's contempt for Christians is therefore contempt for Christ. What do you think should be your response when someone dishonors your Christian faith?

Read James 2:8-13

5. The Royal Law of Love

a) James quotes the Old Testament law, "You shall love your neighbor as yourself" (Leviticus 19:18), which Jesus paired with the great commandment to love God (Deuteronomy 6:5; Matthew 22:36-40). This kind of love (*agape*) unconditionally seeks the other person's highest good. In what way does the sin of partiality violate the commandment to love your neighbor?

b) In v. 8, what does the word "royal" indicate about the law?

c) As discussed in Part I of this lesson, commentators hold various opinions as to what the royal law is. A reasonable view is that the royal law is God's supreme law, including both the gospel and the Mosaic Law fulfilled in Christ. A violation of one aspect of the royal law violates the whole law. In v. 11, what specific example is given?

d) The example in v. 11 cites two of the Ten Commandments (Exodus 20:13-14). These involve intentional sins for which there was no mercy or atoning sacrifice under Mosaic Law, even if the sinner was repentant. What was the punishment for these sins? (See Exodus 21:12 and Leviticus 20:10)

e) Favoritism is only one example of how we break God's law of love. Since any violation of God's law is a violation against all of it, and no one is perfect, every person is guilty and in dire need of God's forgiveness and grace. With this in mind, how would you answer a friend who wrongly asserts that people are righteous in God's eyes if they simply do more good deeds than bad?

6. The Good News of Mercy

Unlike the old Mosaic Law, the gospel offers God's mercy and forgiveness to those who turn to Christ and truly repent of their sins, even intentional sins.

a) In v. 12, James implores Christians to speak and act as those who will be judged by God with mercy under the gospel, the law of liberty. Give an example of the kind of merciful speech and behavior Christians should display toward others out of gratitude for the gospel.

b) In v. 13, on the other hand, if someone fails to show mercy in response to the gospel it is evidence that that person has not truly repented and accepted the gospel, and thus cannot anticipate mercy from God. Try to explain in your own words the danger of rejecting the gospel.

c) In the space below, write the last part of v. 13 and commit it to memory. This is the heart of James' message about partiality.

d) It is interesting to ponder what mercy would look like in the situation back in v. 2. Imagine a similar modern situation, perhaps something you have personally witnessed, and describe what the proper practical response to it should be.

Part III: Personal Application and Growth

Today's lesson points to several important truths that apply to our personal lives. Allow these truths to penetrate your mind, soften your heart, deepen your faith and affect your behavior to help you continually grow in Christ.

1.   Christians must not show favoritism based on external appearances.

Starting this week, how will you show respect to all people who come to your church fellowship, business meetings, and community gatherings, regardless of their outward appearance?

2.   Jesus calls us not to judge wrongly, but to judge rightly.

What steps will you take to become better at discerning good from evil? How will you recognize when you are judging someone wrongly, and what will you do to correct yourself?

3.   We are to show mercy to others because God shows it to us.

What is the first practical thing you will do today to show that your relationships, including how you treat the poor, are under the authority of Christ's royal law of love?

Part IV: Closing Devotion
by Andrew Murray

There may be more than one reader who has felt how little they have lived in accordance with all the teaching of God's word. It appears so difficult to get rid of old habits, to break through the conventionalities of society, to know how to begin and really enter upon a life that can be full of good works, to the glory of God.

Learn to do good works, the works of love, by beginning to do them. However insignificant they appear, do them. A kind word, a little help to someone in trouble, an act of loving attention to a stranger or a poor person, the sacrifice of a seat or a place to someone – practice these things.

Cherish the consciousness that, for Jesus' sake, you are seeking to do what would please Him. Think of the honor and privilege of serving others in love; think of the exquisite joy of growing up into a life of beneficence. Set your heart upon being a vessel suited for the Master's use, ready to every good work.[12]

❧ *Lesson 4* ❧

Doing Good Works

James 2:14-26

Part I: Setting the Stage

Purpose

In this lesson James develops his argument for the connection between faith and good works by considering the examples of Abraham and Rahab, two servants of the Lord. James is consistent with the rest of Scripture in teaching that faith is proved by works. It is important to realize our good works are not the basis of salvation but are the evidence of salvation.

Look for the following application points in this lesson:

1. Faith that does not produce good works is dead.
2. Good intentions to help the poor are made complete by taking action.
3. Saving faith involves our whole being: head, heart, and hands.

James and Paul in Harmony

We have come to one of the most debated passages in Scripture regarding the relationship between faith and works. James says that a person is "justified by works and not by faith alone" (James 2:24). This seems contrary to Paul's teaching that a person is "justified by faith apart from works of the law" (Romans 3:28). Some theologians such as the 16th century Reformer Martin Luther have criticized James for advocating a works-based salvation that contradicts Paul's emphasis on grace.

The apparent tension between James and Paul dissolves when we take a closer look at the way they use the term "justified" (*dikaioo*) in the above verses.[13] James and Paul employ different meanings of the term to address different situations. They speak in complementary rather than contradictory ways.

James is addressing the question of how a believer behaves after being declared righteous by God. He uses the word justified to mean *proved*. When he says believers are justified by works, his point is that their faith is proved or made evident by moral actions that are the natural and inevitable product of genuine faith. Jesus sometimes used the word justified to mean proved (Luke 7:35).

Paul, on the other hand, is concerned with how a believer is declared righteous in the first place. He uses the word justified in a judicial sense of being *declared righteous* (a one-time, permanent change in status before God). When he says believers are justified by faith rather than works of the law, he is saying they are declared righteous by God through faith, not on the basis of their obedience to God's commandments.

Elsewhere when Paul addresses how believers should behave after being declared righteous, he agrees with James that genuine faith is made evident in good works (Ephesians 2:8-10; Titus 3:5-8). The bottom line is that Paul and James are of one accord: we are justified by faith alone, but not by a faith that is alone.

What Is Saving Faith?
James speaks about having a faith that can save. Saving faith is a gift from God, an instrument through which God works. We should not think of saving faith as the ground of our salvation, for the only basis of salvation is the righteousness of Jesus Christ. Saving faith is the means by which we share in Christ's righteousness. Theologian Louis Berkhof defines saving faith:

> "Saving faith may be defined as a certain conviction, wrought in the heart by the Holy Spirit, as to the truth of the gospel, and a hearty reliance (trust) on the promises of God in Christ."[14]

Berkhof also points out three important elements of saving faith. First, one must have intellectual knowledge about the gospel message and believe it is true, especially with regard to sin and redemption in Christ. Second, one must experience emotional assent to the truth of the gospel, feeling it meets an important personal need. Third, there is a volitional element where one surrenders one's will by repenting and trusting in Christ as Lord and Savior, shown by ongoing obedience to God's word. This third element is what distinguishes true believers from unbelievers.

What Are Good Works?

True believers yield their lives to Christ and give evidence of faith by producing an abundance of good works throughout life. A believer's good works serve several purposes including expressing gratitude to God for salvation, earning rewards in heaven, and providing evidence of saving faith now and at the end times.

Good works consist of tangible deeds of mercy and evangelism such as feeding the poor or volunteering at a medical mission clinic. Good works also consist of intangible demonstrations of godly character reflecting the fruit of the Holy Spirit, such as being patient with a difficult person or rejoicing in trials. True believers inevitably produce a combination of good works for God's glory.

Part II: Studying Scripture

Read James 2:14-17

1. The Unity of Faith and Works

a) A person cannot be saved without saving faith, and saving faith always produces good works in obedience to God's word.[15] In v. 14, James imagines someone who wrongly thinks faith can be separated from good works. What are the expected answers to James' rhetorical questions?

b) How does it motivate you to do good works knowing that this lifetime is your only opportunity to produce works that will glorify God at the end times?

c) The Chain of Faith in Lesson 1 showed that the normal course of the Christian life involves trials. Our response to trials is always works of some kind, either good or evil. Our works can be a barometer that indicates whether we are allowing trials to become tests that strengthen our faith, or temptations that weaken our faith. What do your recent actions indicate about how you are responding to trials? What should you be doing to respond better?

2. Useless Faith

a) James presents an illustration of how believers might respond wrongly to the plight of a poor Christian. Note that in the New Testament "brother" or "sister" refers to a believer unless it means a literal sibling. In v. 15, how does James describe the condition of the poor Christian?

b) In v. 16, what is said to the poor Christian? The first of these things is a standard phrase of polite dismissal like "goodbye."

c) The original Greek can be translated either as a wish that the poor person will get his or her own clothing and food ("get yourself warm...") or a wish that it will happen to them ("may you be warm..."). Why is it not enough for us to wish good things in a situation where there are serious physical needs?

d) At the end of v. 16, what is the expected answer to James' rhetorical question? Do you think the question is supposed to apply to the poor person, or "one of you," or both? Why?

e) Read Matthew 25:34-40. Once again we see that James echoes Jesus' teachings. In what practical ways does Jesus expect Christians to behave toward one another as part of the body of Christ, the church?

f) Although the needs of unbelievers are not to be ignored, the New Testament emphasizes the responsibility of Christians to love and care for one another. The underlying principle is to build up the body of Christ, the church, in order to increase its effectiveness in reaching out to serve and bless others. What could go wrong if a local church pours itself out to serve the community but fails to maintain its own vitality? On the other hand, what is wrong with a local church that focuses on its own needs without helping others?

3. Dead Faith

a) In v. 17, faith without works is dead in the sense that it was never living and never a saving faith. A person with dead faith offers lifeless and empty platitudes to a poor person instead of appropriate action. Why do our actions prove that we mean what we say and that our faith is alive?

b) List a variety of ways to help the needy. How well do your actions back up your words when it comes to caring for the needs of poor Christians?

c) Read I John 3:16-18. Christ laid down His life as an expression of love for His people. How are we laying down our lives, figuratively speaking, when we provide for the material needs of poor believers?

Read James 2:18-26

4. Works as the Evidence of Faith

a) In v. 18, James imagines someone who wrongly asserts that one person can have saving faith without good works ("You have faith...") while another person does good deeds apart from faith ("I have works..."). James challenges his imaginary opponent to prove such a false division is possible. Anticipating that his opponent will not succeed, what does James intend to prove instead?

b) In v. 19, apparently the imaginary opponent attempts to offer words instead of works as his proof of faith. What is his brief statement of faith?

c) The imaginary opponent has offered a statement of faith based on the *Shema* recited by devout Jews every morning and evening (Deuteronomy 6:4-5). Read Deuteronomy 6:4 and write it in the space below.

d) Reciting and believing selected statements like "God is one" is good, but it is insufficient proof of saving faith. After all, the fact that there is one God is something that can be truly believed without saving faith. What example does James give? Why does his example confirm that one can have correct knowledge and intellectual belief about God's existence, yet still oppose Him?

e) In v. 20, James calls his imaginary opponent a fool for asserting that saving faith can exist apart from the evidence of good works, and he is determined to set the fool straight. In the Bible a fool is generally someone who rejects God's wisdom; the term is unrelated to intellectual ability. What words would you use to describe James' tone and attitude at this point?

5. An Illustration: Abraham

James supports his argument with the examples of Abraham and Rahab, Old Testament heroes who proved they believed God by acting on their belief. First, James recalls two significant incidents in Abraham's life. He refers to the incidents out of order, assuming the readers know that Abraham's declaration of faith occurred long before the binding of his son Isaac.[16]

a) Read Genesis 22:9-18. When God told Abraham to sacrifice his son Isaac, the son of the covenant, Abraham made the necessary preparations but God intervened to prevent Isaac's death. This was a unique test of faith never to be repeated in history. What covenant promises did God re-affirm because of Abraham's faithful obedience?

b) Re-read James 2:21 and substitute the word "proved" in place of justified or considered righteous. James is commenting on the Genesis 22 episode, saying that Abraham's faith was made evident by his work of offering up Isaac.

c) Read Genesis 15:1-6. Forty or fifty years before the binding of Isaac (fifteen years before Isaac was even born), Abraham (Abram) declared his faith in God's covenant promises. How did God respond to Abraham's faith?

d) In James 2:22-23, what does James say about the relationship between faith and works? James is referring to the episode in Genesis 15 when God counted Abraham as righteous due to his faith.

e) The conclusion in v. 24 tells us that a person's faith is proved by works and not by profession of faith alone. Abraham's declaration of faith led God to count him as righteous, but it was Abraham's works over the decades, including the work of binding Isaac, that gave evidence of his faith. In your own life, what opportunities exist for you to give evidence of your faith?

6. An Illustration: Rahab

James next turns to Rahab as another example of saving faith that produces good works. She is an important figure in redemptive history, for she is a great-great-grandmother of David and an ancestor of Jesus.[17] Rahab lived in Jericho when the Israelites were preparing to enter the Promised Land of Canaan under Joshua's leadership. Jericho was the first city the Israelites needed to conquer.

a) Read Joshua 2:1-4, 8-16. The prostitute Rahab's house was a logical place for strangers to stay without drawing attention to themselves. When the spies' presence was noticed, however, the king sent men to investigate. Rahab hid the spies on her roof, sent the king's men in the wrong direction, and helped the spies escape. Why did the Canaanite Rahab put her trust in the Israelites' God rather than in her king?

b) Scripture portrays most heroes of the faith, including Rahab, as flawed persons who are to be imitated for particular demonstrations of faith, not for everything they say and do. Rahab proved that she truly believed God, wanted to put herself under His lordship and mercy, and had saving faith. In James 2:25, what good works is Rahab remembered for doing? What risks do you suppose she took by doing them?

c) List some ways Rahab and Abraham differed from each other. Why do you think James chose such opposite characters as illustrations? How does Rahab's story reinforce James' earlier exhortation not to judge people on the basis of outward appearances?

d) List some things Rahab and Abraham had in common. What does this tell you about the things that bind believers together in spite of their different situations in life? How will this awareness motivate you to pray for fellow Christians around the world whose lives might be quite different from yours?

Part III: Personal Application and Growth

Today's lesson points to several important truths that apply to our personal lives. Allow these truths to penetrate your mind, soften your heart, deepen your faith and affect your behavior to help you continually grow in Christ.

1. Faith that does not produce good works is dead.

One reason we should be eager to produce good works is that they will be proof of our faith at the end times when God's enemies accuse us. God will point to our lifetime of works as evidence that our faith in Christ was genuine and that we are truly covered by Christ's righteousness. What will you do starting today to be more purposeful about producing good works to bring glory to Christ?

2. Good intentions to help the poor are made complete by taking action.

What action will you take this week to make your behavior more closely match your good intentions to care for the poor, especially poor Christians?

3. Saving faith involves our whole being: head, heart, and hands.

What steps will you take to ensure that you are responding to the gospel with your intellect, emotions and will, and actions?

Part IV: Closing Devotion
by Andrew Murray

We have been saved, not *by* works but *for* good works. How vast the difference. How essential the apprehension of that difference to the health of the Christian life. We are not saved by works we have done, but *for* good works as the fruit and outcome of salvation.

"For we are His workmanship, created in Christ Jesus for good works, which God prepared beforehand, that we should walk in them" (Ephesians 2:10). We have been prepared for the works, and the works prepared for us. Every believer exists to do good works, that in them his or her life may be perfected [made complete], humanity may be blessed, our Father in heaven be glorified.

Let us consider how our new creation for good works is all in Christ Jesus; and abiding in Him, believing on Him, and looking for His strength alone will become the habit of our soul. Let us pray for the Holy Spirit to work the word into the very depths of our consciousness: *Created in Christ Jesus for good works!*[18]

❧ *Lesson 5* ❧

Guiding With Godly Speech

James 3:1-12

Part I: Setting the Stage

Purpose

This lesson points out the powerful influence of words and the negative consequences of ungodly speech. Believers are to serve the Lord by speaking in ways that honor Him. It is important for us to tame our tongues with God's help so that our words bless people and guide them in holiness.

Look for the following application points in this lesson:

1. Serving the Lord involves taming the tongue to bless people.
2. Church leaders have a responsibility to guide wisely with their words.
3. Our words should reveal undivided loyalty to God and Jesus Christ.

The Power of Words

Chances are good you can remember a time when a teacher or friend said something kind to you that has encouraged you to this day. Chances are even better you can recall times when someone made a hurtful remark that caused you to feel discouraged, shamed, angry, or vengeful. People's words matter. Things that are spoken can shape us, sometimes for a lifetime.

James is concerned with the consequences of a believer's words, particularly the words of those who hold leadership roles in the church. It is a sacred trust to be in a position to teach doctrinal truths, motivate people, develop character, and offer spiritual guidance. James is aware that the wrong use of words can mislead God's people into unrighteousness. He has already touched several times on the necessity of carefully guarding our words and the actions that accompany them:

> Be slow to speak from your own understanding; instead, be quick to listen to God's saving word (1:19-21).

> True faith is revealed not by uncontrolled, ungodly speech, but by holy living and deeds of mercy for the defenseless (1:26-27).

> Making a statement of faith, no matter how true it is or how sincerely one believes it, is worthless without being manifested by good deeds (2:14).

A Memorable Theme

James uses the literary device of metonymy, a type of metaphor that employs one thing (in this case, the tongue) to represent a related thing (speech). His use of the device is effective, for his plea to tame the tongue is one of the most memorable themes in his letter.

A series of other metaphors also helps James drive home his point about the power of words. He uses familiar images: a horse and a ship, a forest fire, birds and animals, fresh water and salt water, trees and vines. These images are presented in rapid succession to create a sense of urgency and drama. James warns us to control our speech now, not later when it might be impossible to undo harmful consequences.

Controlling the Tongue

We should learn to use our words carefully, knowing they will have an impact on others. Ponder the wisdom of the following maxims:

- Before speaking, ask: *Is it true? Is it necessary? Is it kind?*
- Remember that not all truth needs to be spoken.
- Words are never neutral; they either bruise or build.
- *Lord, help me bite my tongue before it bites others.*

Ministry leader Joni Eareckson Tada recognizes that her words have the power to be a positive or negative witness to unbelievers. She encourages us to guard our words so we bring light to a spiritually dark world (Philippians 2:14-16):

> "I am very aware that people are watching me. Sure, it's because of my wheelchair and my quadriplegia. But they are really looking at my response to these things. Like some of my neighbors? Ones who don't know Christ? They look at me and are amazed that I don't complain about my wheelchair. And you know what? By God's grace, I don't. Because I don't want them to think, Yeah, she's a Christian, but she grumbles like everybody else; she's no different.
>
> "Look, I want them to be convicted by my uncomplaining spirit... Not complaining speaks volumes about Christ to our dark world. So today, don't complain and you'll shine like a star to your friends in the dark."[19]

Part II: Studying Scripture

Read James 3:1-2

1. A Great Responsibility

a) Think about your pastors and other church teachers and leaders whose words have had a positive influence on you. Who among them was especially helpful in guiding your thinking about God? Why do teachers need to be careful how they use their words and authority?

b) In the local church and at denominational levels, what opportunities to serve involve some type of teaching?

c) In v. 1, what does James say about teaching God's word? Read Matthew 12:36-37. How does James echo Jesus' teaching?

d) The church is responsible for teaching and proclaiming the truth about our Trinitarian God, a subject matter of supreme importance. Why do you think God will judge church leaders and teachers with greater strictness?

2. Mature Teachers

James' warning is not an excuse for believers to avoid being teachers of God's word. It is rather an admonition not to take the task lightly or carelessly.

a) In v. 2, believers are flawed humans who may stumble in sin, but they are still expected to grow in spiritual maturity and live in obedience to God's word. They are to be "perfect" in the sense of being complete, controlling their entire self (words and deeds). When teachers control their speech according to God's word, why do you suppose they are better able to discipline their whole body as well?

b) Read Hebrews 5:12. The author of Hebrews expects believers to become mature in faith so they may be teachers of God's word. Suggest a few things people can do to become more spiritually mature.

c) Read II Peter 2:1-2. False teachers lead people into doctrinal error and often into immorality, particularly sexual immorality. Why would a false teacher's failure to speak the truth about God lead to a failure to behave according to God's truth?

Read James 3:3-8

3. Words That Guide

a) In v. 3, the idea of controlling the body by controlling the tongue is compared to bridling a horse. If you do not have experience with horses, look in a dictionary or ask an equestrian friend how a bridle and bit work together. What is the function of a bit? What is the result when it is used properly? Why is a small thing in the mouth of a thousand pound animal a good analogy?

b) In v. 4, the comparison is with ships. If you do not have experience with boating, look in a dictionary or ask a sailor friend how a rudder works. What is the function of a rudder? What is the result when it is used properly? Why is a small rudder of a large sailing vessel a good analogy?[20]

c) In v. 5a, the point is not just the large size of the body being controlled, but the great result. A small bit, rudder, or tongue determines the direction of the body over a distance and thus can achieve great things. Give an example of something good that can be achieved by the tongue's wise guidance and discipline of the body (an individual person or the church, the body of Christ) over a long period of time.

4. Words That Destroy

a) In v. 5b-6, if a small thing is not used properly it can have a negative effect on a large body. Without being tamed and disciplined, the tongue can bring about widespread destruction. What metaphor does James use? What mental picture or strong feeling does this metaphor evoke in you?

b)   James says the tongue is a world of unrighteousness. What underlying evil desires are revealed when the tongue is used for lies, gossip, cursing, boasting, and put-downs?

c)   Read Proverbs 26:28 and 19:9. What do these proverbs say about a liar's motivation and ultimate destiny?

d)   Why does unrighteous speech often make it easier to do sinful acts?

e)   James says the tongue is set on fire by hell.[21] Therefore, when our words reflect our evil desires, we have unfortunately allowed the devil to influence us. Why do you suppose we allow this to happen and how can we prevent it in the future?

f)   The image of a fire spreading destruction is right on the mark. Sinful speech spreads to the whole person, affecting other aspects of behavior. If we do not purify our speech we will not purify our actions, and the destruction will spread throughout the length and breadth of our lives. How will this fire imagery motivate you on a daily basis to refrain from uttering even a spark of hateful or unkind speech?

g)   If you realize you have spoken words that express your evil desires, what will you do to extinguish the flames and prevent destruction from spreading into all areas of your life?

5. Taming the Tongue

a) In v. 7, what four groups of creatures are mentioned as representing all living things? Where do humans get their authority and ability to rule over other creatures? (See Genesis 1:26-28, the cultural mandate.)

b) We should not take James' hyperbole too literally. His point about taming every creature is that humanity controls a wide range of living creatures. In v. 8, what is one thing humans seem unable to tame? What kind of creature does the description remind you of?

c) Read Genesis 2:15-17 and 3:1-4. In what ways did the serpent Satan misrepresent God's words? What did Jesus later call Satan (John 8:44)?

d) An uncontrolled, untamed tongue is an image of evil itself. Since we cannot tame the tongue by our own strength, what is our only hope (Psalm 141:3)?

Read James 3:9-12

6. Undivided Loyalty

The way we speak is serious business with eternal repercussions. The highest form of speech is blessing God, meaning to give praise, honor, and glory to God. The lowest form of speech is cursing, the opposite of blessing. To curse people is a hateful desire for them to be separated from God and condemned to eternal punishment. Cursing is a judgment only God should make.

a) In v. 9-10, what do you think it means to be made in the likeness of God?[22] Why is cursing other people tantamount to cursing God? Even if we do not use foul language out loud, it is wrong to harbor hateful thoughts. With the help of the Holy Spirit, what changes will you make in the way you think and talk about people you do not like?

b) When someone both blesses God and curses Him by cursing people made in His image, it reveals that the praise to God is not genuine. A person's words come from one source, the heart, and show whether the person has yielded to their evil desires. How would you explain to a new Christian why it is important to consistently honor both God and others with our speech?

c) James uses additional metaphors to illustrate his point that we must have undivided loyalty to God. In v. 11, why is it impossible for a spring bubbling up from one source to produce both fresh (*glykos,* literally "sweet") and bitter (*pikros*) water? Similarly, in v. 12b, why is it impossible for a salt (*halykos*) pond to yield fresh water?

d) In v. 12a, why is it impossible for a tree growing up from one root system to naturally produce different kinds of fruit?

e) Created things should be true to the function for which they were made. A spring is to produce fresh water, a fig tree is to produce healthy figs, and a tongue is to produce abundant blessings. Believers should not speak both praises and curses. To what extent do you share James' righteous outrage over a believer's divided use of the tongue? As Pastor George Stulac asks,

> "Do we today have this same intense reaction – this sense that praising God and cursing people is utterly unthinkable, abhorrent nonsense? ...To accept it or tolerate it, instead of being horrified at it and repenting of it – this must not be! For we, like springs and plants, produce according to our true nature. The production of good fruit

is an evidence of genuine faith and therefore salvation itself. James says to each one of us: Purify your speaking, or show yourself to be an impostor and therefore under judgment."[23]

Part III: Personal Application and Growth

Today's lesson points to several important truths that apply to our personal lives. Allow these truths to penetrate your mind, soften your heart, deepen your faith and affect your behavior to help you continually grow in Christ.

1. Serving the Lord involves taming the tongue to bless people.

Try this simple "Tongue Test." For one week do none of the following: gossip, complain, unfairly criticize, slander, use sarcasm, shift blame, use coarse language, boast, curse, disparage, and deceive. Instead, every time you speak let your words build people up. Allow the Lord to use this test to reveal areas where you need to work on taming your tongue.

2. Church leaders have a responsibility to guide wisely with their words.

What steps will you take to grow in spiritual maturity so you will be better prepared to recognize sound doctrine and support your church leaders in their efforts to teach and guide the congregation wisely?

3. Our words should reveal undivided loyalty to God and Jesus Christ.

The right use of words is a kind of good work that gives evidence of our faith. Find a picture of a spring or healthy fruit tree and place it in a prominent spot in your home or on your computer for a month. Let the picture remind you of the importance of showing your undivided loyalty to God and Christ through your consistent words of blessing to people. What change in your life do you anticipate as a result?

Part IV: Closing Devotion
by Andrew Murray

The need is great to teach all Christians to be ready to every good work, to teach them what an essential part of the Christian life good works are.

Good works are not merely to be done in token of our gratitude, or as a proof of the sincerity of our faith, or as a preparation for heaven. They are all this, but they are a great deal more. They are the object for which we have been redeemed. They alone are evidence that humans have been restored to their original destiny of working as God works. When others are won to Christ, God's servants share in the joy in which our blessed Lord found His reward.

In becoming imitators of God and working in love, even as Christ loved us and gave Himself for us, we have the very image and likeness of God restored in us. Good works are of the essence of the Divine life in us.

God grant that the teachers of the Church may be faithful to lead every believer to live entirely devoted to the work of God.[24]

✎ *Lesson 6* ✑
Seeking God's Wisdom for Holy Living

James 3:13-4:12

Part I: Setting the Stage

Purpose

This lesson explores the practical difference it makes for Christians, servants of the Lord, to follow God's wisdom as opposed to the world's counterfeit wisdom. It is important for us to grasp the truth that earthly, worldly wisdom leads to discord and every vile practice, while heavenly wisdom leads to peace and righteousness.

Look for the following application points in this lesson:

1. We are to allow God's wisdom to guide our thoughts and actions.
2. God is the one who gives us the grace needed to resist worldliness.
3. Love for God and one another is the basis for holy living.

What Is Wisdom?

One of God's attributes or characteristics is His wisdom. Wisdom can generally be defined as the application of good sense while making decisions based on knowledge and experience. God's wisdom represents the ultimate good sense, for God always sets forth the best goals and the best ways to achieve those goals. His wisdom is most clearly revealed in His plan of redemption for the world in Jesus Christ.

God shares His wisdom with believers who ask for it; it is a good gift from heaven (James 1:5, 17). Christians who live by God's wisdom will give evidence of it in their thoughts, words, and deeds. Their whole lives will reflect God's perspective as they seek His will and live in practical obedience to His word.

The Darkness of Worldly Wisdom

A classic depiction of the disastrous results of the world's wisdom is found in *Pilgrim's Progress,* written by the 17th century English Puritan preacher, John Bunyan.[25] His allegory about the faith journey of a man named Christian remains one of the most widely read books in the English language.

At one point in the story Christian and his traveling companion Faithful must pass through the town of Vanity ruled by Beelzebub (Satan). The entire town has become a year-round fair where everything is for sale: food, jewels, houses, jobs, titles, sex, slaves, children, bodies, blood... everything. Injustice and all kinds of immorality are rampant, including adultery and murder.

As Christian and Faithful walk through the town, their refusal to participate in the demonic worldliness of Vanity Fair creates a disturbance. They are jailed and tortured for holding on to their faith in God's truth. Christian escapes and continues his journey only after witnessing his friend's horrible execution and glorious entry into heaven.

The episode is a timeless and relevant commentary on the vile results of unchecked worldliness. The problem continues today, confronting us in daily news reports, pressure to conform to the world, and in broken lives all around us. Without God's absolute morality, all evil is ultimately permissible.

The Light of God's Wisdom

In contrast to the dark and deadly results of worldly wisdom, divine wisdom brings life and light. One of the best examples of what happens when believers follow heavenly wisdom is found in Luke's description of the mother church at Jerusalem (Acts 2:42-47). He reports that in the days after Pentecost the church was characterized by:

- Unity and devotion to the apostles' teaching about Christ
- Grace, fellowship, communion, and prayer
- Power revealed in the apostles' healing miracles
- Generosity and no poverty
- Rapid increase in the number of believers

The church was certainly not perfect in all its particulars and faced serious challenges to its unity, but the leaders relied on heavenly wisdom. When the apostles needed to take better care of widows in the church, for instance, they appointed seven deacons full of the Holy Spirit and wisdom (Acts 6:3). Then and now, God's wisdom is essential for holy living.

Part II: Studying Scripture

Read James 3:13-18

1. Who Is Wise?

a) Take a moment to ponder James' self-searching question, "Who is wise and understanding among you?" What would you say is the difference between being wise and having understanding or knowledge? In what ways do these traits enhance each other?

b) What has James already taught about obtaining wisdom (1:5)?

c) In v. 13, wisdom is proved by godly living. A person who is truly wise and full of understanding will show it in words and actions that please the Lord. What does it mean to conduct oneself in the meekness or humility of wisdom? Why do humility and wisdom go together?

2.   Earthly vs. Heavenly Wisdom

True wisdom comes from heaven above. There is a counterfeit wisdom that comes from below, but counterfeit wisdom is not really wise at all.

a)   In v. 14-16, what are some sinful characteristics and behaviors of those who follow earthly, worldly wisdom? Notice the progression from bad to worse, from selfish character to every evil deed.

b)   In v. 15, where does earthly wisdom come from? It is not difficult to see why earthly wisdom leads to quarrels, chaos, and general lawlessness when we consider its source.

c)   In v. 17-18, list some godly characteristics and behaviors of those who listen to divine wisdom. Notice the progression from a pure heart to an abundance of good works and righteousness.

d)   God's wisdom leads to peace while Satan's counterfeit earthly wisdom brings discord. Why do you think individuals or societies that say they want world peace often reject God's wisdom, the only source of peace?

e)   Read Matthew 5:9. James echoes Jesus' teaching in the Beatitudes that peacemaking is a family trait among God's people. How would acquaintances in your life say you are doing at exhibiting the family resemblance? What will you do to sow more godly peace in your family and community?

f)   Read Galatians 5:19-25. Paul points out the stark contrast between a life guided by the Holy Spirit and a life guided by worldly wisdom. Name some similarities between what Paul and James are saying.

Read James 4:1-6

3.   The Problem of Worldliness

James asks another self-searching question, "What causes quarrels (literally "wars") and what causes fights among you?" The answer lies within us. James says the cause is *hedon* (literally "pleasures"), translated as passions, lust, or desires. When we respond to our self-indulgent, hedonistic desires by turning to worldly wisdom, the results are devastating.

a)   In v. 2a-b, James' point is made clear when the punctuation forms a literary couplet in which the second line restates the first (see below). Why is coveting (envying what someone else has) a fitting description of our heart problem?

> *"You desire and do not have, so you murder.*
> *You covet and cannot obtain, so you fight and quarrel."*

b)   The Ten Commandments are a summary of God's moral law. The tenth commandment is a prohibition against coveting (Exodus 20:17). Why is coveting an offense against God? How would you explain to an unbeliever why the inner heart condition of coveting belongs in the same category with outward crimes like murder, adultery, stealing, and false testimony?

c)   In v. 2c-3, why do people fail to have what they desire, even when they ask God in prayer?

d)   In v. 4, James' tone is harsh. People who are friends with the world are "adulteresses" who are unfaithful to God. The world (*kosmos*) here means humanity or man-made human systems. God loves humanity, but He does not love our worldliness, our devotion to the things of this world. Give an example of how friendship with the world means enmity with God.

e) In v. 5, the proof text is unknown and might be a composite of verses. It is unclear whether "spirit" refers to the Holy Spirit or a worldly human spirit, and whether spirit is the subject or object. Translators handle it in different ways: (1) God is jealous about our worldly spirit; (2) Our worldly spirit creates envy in us; or (3) God desires the Holy Spirit for us. In any event, we should choose God over worldliness. What is an area in your life where you still struggle against worldliness? Why do you think it is so difficult to overcome?

f) Read John 17:14-15. What does Jesus pray for regarding His followers? What do you think it means for Christians to be *in* the world but not *of* the world? Why is it difficult to maintain that distinction?

4. The Remedy for Worldliness

a) In v. 6, what does the proof text (quoted from Proverbs 3:34, Septuagint version) say is God's solution to our enmity with Him?

b) God takes the initiative in resolving our enmity. How is God's grace (His unmerited favor toward sinful people) revealed in the person and saving work of Jesus Christ?

c) The humble are restored to friendship with God through Christ. Why do you suppose the arrogant fail to benefit?

d) Read Matthew 7:7-8; John 14:13-14; and I John 5:14-15. What should Christians do when they desire to attain something? What promises are given to them? What will you do to ensure you are asking for things in accordance with Christ's will and not with a worldly spirit?

Read James 4:7-10

5. Loving God

James gives several brief commands to help us focus on what we should be doing to deepen our relationship with God. Love for God is the basis of holy living and peaceful relationships with others.

a) Submit to God. Submission is voluntary obedience that shows our respect for authority, like Jesus' submission to His parents (Luke 2:51). Why is our submission to God's will the only acceptable response to His grace?

b) Resist the devil. The fact that Satan is under Jesus' control should embolden us to resist him. In v. 7b, what promise does God make?

c) Draw near to God. In v. 8a, what promise does God make to those who seek Him? Read Hebrews 11:6. What must we believe in order to draw near to God?

d) Cleanse and purify yourself. Christians are responsible for responding to God's grace with their whole undivided being. With the help of the Holy Spirit we are to outwardly clean up our behavior (hands) and inwardly keep God as our focus (hearts). What does it look like to be holy, meaning set apart for God, in everyday matters of finances, entertainment, work, and relationships?

e) Repent. True repentance is more than remorse at being caught. It includes heartfelt sorrow for sin, confession, taking responsibility for the consequences, and resolving not to repeat the sin. Why are worldly joy and laughter out of place when we are truly mourning our sinfulness?

f) Humble yourself. Humility means reliance on God and is the opposite of being self-righteous and prideful. In v. 10, what promise does God make to the humble? Read Matthew 23:12. How does James echo Jesus' teaching?

Read James 4:11-12

6. Loving One Another

Our loving relationship with God should overflow into our relationships with one another. James again warns us to guard our speech, particularly when we are tempted to slander other believers. Slander is a false verbal statement that damages a person's reputation. It is a form of judging due to envy and is the result of listening to wisdom from below, from the devil (*diabolos*, meaning "slanderer" or "accuser").

a) In v. 11, when we judge or speak evil against a fellow Christian, what else are we judging?

b) Slander violates the royal law of love discussed in Lesson 3, including the ninth commandment not to bear false witness (Exodus 20:16). Those who commit slander act as if they are above God's law, but God is the only true Lawgiver and Judge. In v. 12, what does God have the power to do? Why should this motivate us to speak in love, not out of envy?

c) In your experience, what damage can occur in a church fellowship due to slander? How can a deep understanding of God's love and grace keep believers from speaking against each other, building each other up instead?

Part III: Personal Application and Growth

Today's lesson points to several important truths that apply to our personal lives. Allow these truths to penetrate your mind, soften your heart, deepen your faith and affect your behavior to help you continually grow in Christ.

1. We are to allow God's wisdom to guide our thoughts and actions.

When you seek God's wisdom each day, what will you do to make certain that your requests are in agreement with the Lord's Prayer Jesus taught His disciples (Matthew 6:9-10):

> *Hallowed be Thy name...* Does your request glorify God's name?
> *Thy kingdom come...* Does your request further God's kingdom?
> *Thy will be done...* Does your request harmonize with God's will?

2. God is the one who gives us the grace needed to resist worldliness.

By God's grace, what changes will you make this week to strengthen your friendship with God and reject worldliness in your life?

3. Love for God and one another is the basis for holy living.

What practical steps will you take to keep from speaking unkind words to other Christians, and instead speak loving words that encourage them?

Part IV: Closing Devotion
by Andrew Murray

As an apple tree or a vine is planted solely for its fruit, so the great purpose of our redemption is that God may have us for His work and service. We must seek all wisdom and strength from God alone. And we shall boldly give ourselves, as those who are responsible for the use of that wisdom and strength, to the diligence and the sacrifice and the effort needed for a life bearing fruit in every good work.

No works can have any worth but as they come of love. It is love that gives us the patience that refuses to give up the unthankful or the hardened. It is love that reaches and overcomes the most hopeless. Both in ourselves and those for whom we labor, love is the power for work. Let us love as Christ loved us.

Pray for the spirit of love. Give yourself to a life of love, to think how you can love those around you by praying for them, by serving them, by laboring for their wellbeing. Faith working by love in Christ Jesus, this alone produces much.[26]

Lesson 7

Relying on God in Humility

James 4:13-5:12

Part I: Setting the Stage

Purpose

This lesson takes a candid look at what happens when money gets between people and God. Wealth tends to draw people's hearts away from reliance on God and can lead to abuse of power. The poor may envy the rich and be tempted not to trust Christ for justice. It is important for us, the Lord's devoted servants, to humbly rely on Him in all economic circumstances.

Look for the following application points in this lesson:

1. Remember that your future plans are subject to God's sovereign will.
2. Avoid the sins of the arrogant rich: self-reliance, hoarding, defrauding, complacent self-indulgence, and oppression of the poor.
3. Wait patiently for God's justice until Christ returns.

God's Attitude Toward Money

One of God's gracious blessings for His faithful covenant people is abundant living. Abundant living includes spiritual blessings from God, His provision for our needs, and sometimes considerable material wealth. Wealth in itself is not a good or bad thing. Some of Scripture's greatest heroes of the faith were extremely wealthy such as Abraham, Job, David, and Solomon. On the other hand, not all of God's faithful people prosper materially.

Whether we have much or little, God holds us accountable for being good stewards. He evaluates the way we obtain, save, spend, and use money and possessions. We are to get wealth honestly, not by defrauding, stealing, or cheating. We should use wealth carefully, not for self-indulgent luxury, waste, or corruption of justice.

Our Heart Attitude

The problem with acquiring wealth is that it tends to change one's attitude toward God. It can make people feel prideful and self-reliant, thinking they do not need to depend on God because money will solve their problems. They might base their self-worth on the size of their bank account. Wealth also wields power over others and can lead to corruption. As Paul puts it, "the love of money is a root of all kinds of evils" (I Timothy 6:10).

James encourages us to cultivate a humble heart that relies on God whether we are rich or poor. Most of his readers may have been poor, perhaps due to persecution, and could not defend themselves from the exploitation of the wicked rich. James advises them to be patient and persevere in faith. Christ will one day return to avenge any wrongs done to them. In the meantime they should not envy the rich, for the destiny of the unrepentant wicked rich is certain doom.

In the End

Psalm 73 is a source of comfort to those who have been unfairly oppressed and are awaiting God's justice. The psalmist talks about how he envied the rich until he turned to God in worship and was shown their terrible destiny:

> "But as for me, my feet had almost stumbled, my steps had nearly slipped. For I was envious of the arrogant when I saw the prosperity of the wicked... When I thought how to understand this, it seemed to me a wearisome task, until I went into the sanctuary of God; then I discerned their end. Truly you set them in slippery places; you make them fall to ruin. How they are destroyed in a moment, swept away utterly by terrors!" (Psalm 73:2-19)

All wrongs will be made right at the end times when Christ returns as the great Judge. Theologians calls Christ's second coming the *parousia* (pronounced pair-uh-SEE-uh, literally "presence"). The return of Christ at the end times will be a sudden, visible, bodily event resulting in final judgment, with eternal punishment for unbelievers and eternal reward for believers.[27]

The timing of the *parousia* is uncertain and each generation lives with the expectation that Jesus *might* return in their lifetime. If He does not, there is no need to think He has been delayed, for He will come at exactly the right time. The important thing is for us to live in such a way as to be prepared to meet Jesus whether at His return or upon our death. Jesus said, "Therefore you also must be ready, for the Son of Man is coming at an hour you do not expect" (Matthew 24:44).

Part II: Studying Scripture

Read James 4:13-17

Here we have an illustration of arrogant, self-reliant merchants who fail to acknowledge that God is the source of their prosperity and is sovereign over their lives. James addresses these ungodly rich as if they have been called to a court hearing.

1. A Warning for the Arrogant Rich

a) In v. 13, the hearing begins with a summons, "Come now, you who say..." This statement is reminiscent of Old Testament prophets who employed lawsuit and courtroom language to get people's attention. Why do you think James uses this format and what do you think he hopes to accomplish by it?

b) Re-read v. 13 by inserting the name of a modern city and a popular trade product that could result in impressive sales profits. What are some similarities between doing business today and two thousand years ago?

c) Although it is smart to create a business plan for a new venture, we must not assume that we are in control of the future. The plan in v. 13 does not acknowledge God's sovereignty or the possibility of contingencies or unforeseen events. What do you imagine could go wrong with the plan? How do your own financial plans reveal your humility toward God?

d) In v. 14, life is a vanishing mist or vapor. We do not know for sure what life holds for us. Find other images in the passages below that allude to the uncertainty, brevity, and swiftness of life:

Job 7:6-9 _____

Job 9:25-26 _____

Job 14:2 _____

Psalm 102:3, 11 _____

e) In v. 15-17, the conditional phrase "if the Lord wills" should be part of our thinking when we make future plans. Of course, we do not need to wonder if the Lord wills something already made clear in Scripture, such as our duty to care for the poor, but we must seek His will in carrying out the details. What does James say about knowing we should rely on God but failing to do so?

Read James 5:1-6

2. Punishment for the Unrepentant Rich

a) In v. 1, a second hearing begins with a summons, "Come now, you rich..." This time James uses an illustration of wicked landowners who are in danger of condemnation at the final judgment. They will face "miseries," an allusion to hell.[28] How will they respond to their punishment?

b) The response of the condemned rich is a hopeless type of mourning unlike the weeping of repentance in 4:9. Read Matthew 25:41, 46; and II Thessalonians 1:9. What fate awaits the wicked?

c) Read Luke 16:19-31. In Jesus' parable, the poor man Lazarus is comforted in heaven when he dies. On the other hand, what torment does the rich man experience in hell? Why do you suppose the rich man did not alleviate Lazarus' suffering during life?[29] What is arrogant about the rich man's request for Lazarus to help him and his brothers after death?

d) Sometimes people today joke about wanting to spend eternity in hell because they say that is where their friends will be. They wrongly imagine that after death the wicked will continue to enjoy the selfish pleasures of this life. How will you respond to someone who treats Scripture's warnings about eternal punishment like a joke?

3. Evidence Convicting the Rich

a) In v. 2-3, the first evidence against the unrepentant rich is hoarding. What do various types of goods like food, fabric, wood, and metal look like when they deteriorate due to neglect?[30] What happens to their usefulness? What is wrong with allowing things to go to waste rather than be used for their created purpose?

b) In v. 3, it is ironic that the owner allows his possessions to decay during his life, and those possessions then cause the owner's decay after life.[31] This is poetic justice. Explain how the punishment fits the crime.

c) Read Luke 12:16-21. In Jesus' parable of the rich fool, what is the real problem with accumulating wealth? What do you think is the difference between saving and hoarding? How should a person use wealth (see Luke 12:33-34)?

d) In v. 4, the second evidence James presents against the unrepentant rich is defrauding. Failure to pay daily wages to a laborer could mean starvation for his family (Deuteronomy 24:14-15). Why is it a form of defrauding today when we do not pay what we owe someone for services rendered, for a credit purchase, or for a loan that is due?

e) The workers' cries reach the mighty Lord of hosts, Lord *Sabaoth* ("army"). God commands an army of angels more powerful than any human military force. Abused workers have the ultimate ally in God who is willing and able to avenge all wrongs. How would this comfort the poor among James' readers?

f) In v. 5, the third evidence against the unrepentant rich is complacent self-indulgence. What will be their fate at the final Day of Judgment?

g) In v. 6, the fourth evidence against the unrepentant rich is oppression of the poor. The poor are often called righteous in Scripture, for they must rely on God (Psalm 37:16). The wealthy can hire lawyers and initiate prolonged lawsuits that bankrupt the poor who cannot afford to defend themselves in court or stand up to retaliation. The rich can obstruct justice by bribing or influencing corrupt judges, witnesses, and legislators. What does James harshly accuse the wicked rich of doing either figuratively or literally?

Read James 5:7-12

4. The Patience of God's People

a) In v. 7, the poor are to wait for justice until Christ returns. The word for patience (*makrothymia*) means to wait with self-restraint. What is James' example of someone who is patient? What would be encouraging about knowing that God inevitably sends the harvest in due time (Genesis 8:22)?[32]

b) In v. 8-9, the prospect of the final judgment should motivate poor believers to develop an inner strength that helps them remain unmoved by trouble. They are not to grumble against one another in their distress. Suggest some ways believers might develop this kind of patience and strength.

c) In v. 10, the prophets are an example of those who patiently and faithfully endured suffering (Matthew 5:11-12). For instance, God's prophet Jeremiah was persecuted by his countrymen for delivering unpopular prophecies from God. List what the following verses tell us about Jeremiah's suffering:

Jeremiah 20:2   _____
Jeremiah 32:3   _____
Jeremiah 38:6-9 _____

5. The Perseverance of God's People

a) In v. 11, James refers to Job as an example of persevering in faith despite great suffering and loss. Perseverance (*hypomone*) means endurance with strength. List what the following verses tell us about Job's perseverance:

Job 1:20-22 _____

Job 19:25-27 _____

Job 23:11-12 _____

Job 42:2-6 _____

b) How does God show compassion and mercy to Job at the end (Job 42:10)?

c) Critics complain that Job's happy ending is not the experience of most suffering believers. Such criticism, though, misses the point that Job's restoration in this lifetime symbolizes the glorious way God will set all things right at the end times. Pastor D.A. Carson puts it this way:

> "The blessings that Job experiences at the end are not cast as rewards that he has earned by his faithfulness under suffering. The epilogue simply describes the blessings as the Lord's free *gift*. The Lord is not nasty or capricious. He may for various reasons withdraw his favor, but his love endures forever. In that sense, *the epilogue is the Old Testament equivalent to the New Testament anticipation of a new heaven and a new earth. God is just and will be seen to be just.*"[33] [Italics added]

6. The Loyalty of God's People

James' warning against swearing does not refer to cursing or vulgar language, as bad as those are, nor to legal oaths in court, for God Himself took binding oaths. Rather, it prohibits evasion of the truth by swearing on something less than God such as stars and angels or an earthly entity like Jerusalem.

a) In v. 12, why do you think an oppressed believer would be tempted to evade the truth? Give an example of the ways people today try to avoid being entirely honest.

b) Swearing by anything other than God as a witness to the truth is a form of idolatry. It gives a created thing the authority that belongs only to God. Why would James warn against idolatry, divided loyalty, and God's ensuing judgment, at the climax of his discussion about faithful perseverance?

c) Read Matthew 5:33-37 and 12:36-37. What is similar between Jesus' teaching and what James is saying? How will you take it to heart?

Part III: Personal Application and Growth

Today's lesson points to several important truths that apply to our personal lives. Allow these truths to penetrate your mind, soften your heart, deepen your faith and affect your behavior to help you continually grow in Christ.

1. Remember that your future plans are subject to God's sovereign will.

What steps will you take starting today to develop the habit of seeking God's will and guidance when you make plans?

2. Avoid the sins of the arrogant rich: self-reliance, hoarding, defrauding, complacent self-indulgence, and oppression of the poor.

Try this simple "Stuff Test." This week ask yourself if each of your possessions meets one of the following criteria: *Is it useful? Is it beautiful? Is it meaningful?* What is your plan for parting with possessions that do not meet at least one of these guidelines? How will the poor benefit from your cleaning out?

3.   Wait patiently for God's justice until Christ returns.

How will you avoid the temptation to grumble against God or one another during times of hardship? What will you do to establish your heart in godliness so you are ready for the final Day of Judgment upon Christ's return?

Part IV: Closing Devotion
by Andrew Murray

In the present world riches are often God's reward for diligence and enterprise. But their danger consists in their being of this world, in their drawing off the heart from the living God and heavenly treasures.

The gospel meets the desire for riches by the command to be rich in good works. By abounding in good works we lay up for ourselves treasures in heaven: in relieving the poor, in helping the lost, in bringing the gospel to others.

The person who is rich in money may become rich in good works by following the instructions Scripture lays down. The money must not be given as from an owner, but a steward who administers the Lord's money, with prayer for His guidance. Nor with any confidence in its power or influence, but in deep dependence on Him who alone can make it a blessing.

As with all Christian work, our money-giving has value alone from the spirit in which it is done, the spirit of Christ Jesus.[34]

❧ *Lesson 8* ❧
Praying for One Another
James 5:13-20

Part I: Setting the Stage

Purpose
This final lesson focuses on the central role of prayer in the lives of those who serve the Lord. We are to put our faith into practice by praying for ourselves and others in all kinds of circumstances. It is essential that Christians intercede in prayer for one another, especially during difficult times such as sickness, and pray in Jesus' name in accordance with His will.

Look for the following application points in this lesson:

1. We should pray in all kinds of circumstances.
2. We are to pray for each other's burdens in accordance with God's will.
3. Christians have a responsibility to care for one another's souls.

So Many Ways to Use Words
The godly use of the tongue has been a major theme throughout the book of James. The way we speak to people and God reveals our spiritual condition and can influence others. Consider some of the various ways James has approached the subject so far:

- Pray for God's wisdom.
- Be slow to speak from your own understanding.
- Bridle your tongue.
- Do not favor the rich or offer platitudes to the poor.

- Guide wisely with your words.
- Prove your statement of faith with good works.
- Use your words for blessing, not cursing.
- Avoid quarrels caused by worldliness.
- Refrain from speaking against fellow believers.
- Do not boast in arrogance.
- Speak honestly.

The Prayer of Faith

In his closing verses James encourages us to pray, sing, and confess our sins. He also highlights a particular use of words in prayer; that is, praying for healing. The sick are to ask the church elders to pray in faith, and all the believers are to share in confession of sin and prayers for healing.

We need to be careful at this point to understand that we live in a fallen world and that illness and death are still part of the human experience. There is no special "prayer of faith" that brings healing. Even if God grants healing in answer to prayer in one case, in His sovereignty He may choose not to heal in another case. Theologian Wayne Grudem writes that our response is to be the same in all situations:

> "When God chooses not to heal, even though we ask him for it, then it is right that we 'give thanks in all circumstances' (I Thess. 5:18) and realize that God can use sickness to draw us closer to himself and to increase in us obedience to his will... Therefore God can bring increased sanctification to us through illness and suffering... The point is that in everything God should receive glory and our joy and trust in him should increase."[35]

Watching Out for Each Other

James ends his letter with a call to action. He has lovingly addressed the readers as "brothers" fifteen times in this letter, a term that includes sisters in Christ, and his loving concern is made evident by his desire for Christians to get involved when someone in their midst turns to sin. We may prefer to look the other way, but we are called to care for one another's souls. This is no time for spiritual complacency.

Christianity was never intended to be practiced in isolation. We are members of the same body of Christ, united with each other because we are united with Christ. Christians have a corporate responsibility to pray for each other, confess their sins to one another, watch over each other's spiritual welfare, and hold each other accountable.

When James speaks about the danger of someone wandering from the "truth," he is talking about the truth of the gospel of Jesus Christ. That gospel truth is what saves our souls from eternal death and secures the forgiveness of sins. It is fitting that James uses eschatological (end times) language emphasizing the approaching Day of Judgment, for the gospel is the key to our blessed eternal destiny.

Part II: Studying Scripture

Read James 5:13-18

1. Pray in All Circumstances

a)   In v. 13, what should those who are suffering or in trouble do?

b)   The Greek word for suffering or trouble (*kakopatheo*) refers to all kinds of afflictions and trials. It is the word used for the prophets' suffering (James 5:10) and Paul's imprisonment (II Timothy 2:9). What kind of trouble are you enduring at present? In what way does your personal prayer life lighten your burden?

c)   Think of someone in your church who is discouraged because of the troubles they are facing. In what practical way will you encourage him or her to maintain a strong personal prayer life?

d) In v. 13, what should those who are cheerful do?

e) The Greek word for cheerful (*euthymeo*) implies an inner sense of well-being and courage regardless of circumstances.[36] Paul used the same word to encourage fellow travelers to take heart as they faced shipwreck on the way to Rome (Acts 27:22, 25). God is the only source of this inner contentment. Describe a time when you or others spontaneously sang praises in response to stress or trouble. Why does music often express feelings better than talking?

f) Singing praise to God is a form of prayer. When we sing psalms, hymns, and praise songs during a worship service, we are praying out loud.[37] How will this perspective motivate you to sing more enthusiastically in church? And how will this perspective help you see your choir or worship team as co-worshipers rather than performers?

2. Pray for One Another

a) In v. 14, what should the sick do? Here we see a practical example of how an individual's submission to the local church works together with the church's submission to the Lord.

b) Believers should offer intercessory prayer in the Lord's name, asking for God's will to be done. This means God will grant healing only if it is His will. How can this understanding comfort Christians who feel guilty that their heartfelt prayers do not result in someone being healed?

c) The elders' prayers for healing were to be accompanied by anointing with oil, symbolizing the elders' faith in God's healing power.[38]

There is some debate in the church as to whether such anointing was a practice for the apostolic age only, or whether it is permissible or necessary today. Scripture gives no record of Jesus healing with oil but His disciples did so at times (Mark 6:13). Ask your pastor about your church's position on anointing with oil for healing purposes.

d) In v. 15, no special "prayer of faith" is in view. The assurance that the prayers of the elders will save the sick must be taken in the context of the previous verse invoking the Lord's name. Healing, whether physical or spiritual, is up to God. How do you feel knowing that our sovereign God, not you or the church elders, is in control?

3. Pray with Power

a) In v. 15-16, a believer whose sin and guilt are manifested in sickness should confess with genuine repentance and ask the church to pray. In doing so the believer demonstrates saving faith that carries an assurance of pardon. Accepting God's forgiveness may have a healing effect on the believer's body and soul. Why might people be hesitant to confess their sins to their church elders or others in the church? What would it take to establish trust?

b) Why do you think people do not always enjoy the benefits that flow from God's forgiveness of sin, such as a clean conscience? If people continue to be burdened by guilt, what have they failed to understand about the gospel?

c) Scripture often describes a faithful and godly person as righteous. The righteous pray in accordance with God's will. With this in mind, explain in your own words why the prayers of a righteous person have great power.

d) In v. 17-18, the prophet Elijah is an example of a righteous man whose prayers were effective (I Kings 17 and 18). Elijah achieved dramatic results when he prayed about rain in accordance with God's will. How should the fact that Elijah was an ordinary human embolden our prayer efforts?

Read James 5:19-20

4. Hold to the Truth

a) In v. 19, how should believers respond when someone in the church wanders (*planao,* from which we get "planet") from the truth of God's word?

b) In v. 20, what are two results in the life of a sinner who is brought back to God's word? Note that the rescuer is an instrument in God's hands, for God is the one who brings about salvation and forgiveness.

c) Read Ezekiel 3:17-20. What responsibility do God's people have?

d) Read Galatians 6:1. With what attitude should believers confront a sinner in their midst? Why is it essential to remember that a primary goal of church discipline is to restore the sinner to the fellowship?

e) Read Matthew 18:15-17. What is Jesus' advice when one Christian sins against another? Remember that church discipline is for the benefit of the sinner's soul and the health of the church, not to be undertaken lightly.

Read Acts 15:6-21 (The Council at Jerusalem)

5.   Reach Out in Grace

An example of the gracious way James cared for the Lord's people is seen in his role at the Jerusalem Council in A.D. 49. The main issue at stake was whether Gentile Christians must observe Jewish ceremonial law in order to be saved, as Judaizers insisted, or if Gentiles were covered by grace, as Paul and Barnabas taught. The apostles were asked to make an official decision.

a)   The apostle Peter rightly argued that placing the burden of ceremonial law on Gentile Christians would be to reject the grace of the gospel. Give a modern example of trying to earn salvation by adding one's own efforts to Christ's gracious work. How can we avoid the error of trying to earn our salvation?

b)   James presided at the Council. He based his final ruling on God's word, quoting the prophet Amos who foretold that Gentile Christians would be part of God's people (Amos 9:11-12). Since it was God's plan to include Gentiles and He had already sent the Holy Spirit to them as He had to the Jews, in v. 19 what was James' conclusion about the need to observe ceremonial law?[39]

c)   Why was it important for James to ground his decision in the context of Scripture? When a dispute arises in your local church, what will you do to encourage church leaders to search Scripture before making any decisions?

d)   The need to extend grace to others has been a consistent message throughout the book of James. Perhaps James emphasizes grace (God's unmerited favor) because he personally experienced its transforming power. The grace of Jesus Christ changed him forever from a doubter to a believer. Write a brief sentence summarizing your own faith journey. When did you first begin to understand God's grace?

e) Examine your life with regard to how you are currently serving the Lord by serving His people. What will you do to serve more whole-heartedly and with more grace? What do you think is the best way to avoid burn-out and maintain the heart of a devoted servant throughout your life?

6. Closing Thoughts

a) The book of James has been called the "Ouch!" book because it is so pointed.[40] James may seem harsh at times, but he is determined to prevent us from taking a theoretical or careless approach to serving the Lord. How would you describe your reaction to James' bluntness?

b) James practiced what he preached as he persevered in faith through turbulent years in Jerusalem. In A.D. 62 he was killed by Jewish religious authorities who placed him on top of the Temple and demanded he recant his faith in Christ to the large Passover crowds. When James instead boldly proclaimed Jesus as the Messiah, he was pushed off the Temple, stoned, and beaten to death.[41] How will James' life and death inspire you to serve the Lord without fear?

c) Take a moment to look at the application points at the end of each lesson up to now (see the complete list in Appendix A). Consider what the points say about being a servant of the Lord. Which points are most important to you and why? How will you use these points to remind you in the future of what you have learned from your study of the book of James?

d) Ask the Holy Spirit to continue to apply God's word to your heart and mind so that the insights you have gained will be a lasting blessing to you and others.

Part III: Personal Application and Growth

Today's lesson points to several important truths that apply to our personal lives. Allow these truths to penetrate your mind, soften your heart, deepen your faith and affect your behavior to help you continually grow in Christ.

1. We should pray in all kinds of circumstances.

Starting today, what will you do to strengthen your prayer life? If you are not already doing so, how will you include in your prayers the elements of the acronym ACTS:

> *Adoration for who God is and what He has done*
> *Confession of your sins*
> *Thanksgiving for God's provision and blessings in Christ*
> *Supplication for things that you and others need*

2. We are to pray for each other's burdens in accordance with God's will.

What will you do to increase your efforts at intercessory prayer for those in your congregation who are suffering, particularly those who are sick?

3. Christians have a responsibility to care for one another's souls.

Who in your life will you help bring back to the truth of God's word, perhaps by encouraging them to seek counsel from your pastor or elders? What practical steps will you take to be better equipped to disciple someone?

Part IV: Closing Devotion
by Andrew Murray

Nothing will bring God so near, will test and strengthen our faith, and make us know we are fellow workers with God, as when we receive an answer to our prayers for individuals. It will quicken in us the new and blessed consciousness that we indeed have power with God. Let every worker seek to exercise this grace of taking up and praying for individual souls.

Count upon an answer. We have confidence of being heard if we ask anything according to God's will. The Holy Spirit will lead us, if we yield ourselves to be led by Him, to the souls God would have us take as our special care, and for which the grace of faith and persevering prayer will be given us.

God will hear the one who asks life for them who sin. Let the wonderful promise stir us and encourage us to intercession, as one of the most blessed among the good works in which we can serve God and people.[42]

Appendix A
Application Points

A list of the personal application points at the end of each lesson.

Lesson 1: Persevering with Joy

1. Christians are to serve Jesus Christ with the heart of a devoted servant.
2. We should ask God for wisdom to deal with trials.
3. We should consider it all joy when we face trials because trials serve a redemptive purpose for Christians.

Lesson 2: Obeying God's Word

1. Christians should be advised by God's saving word.
2. We are to control our anger and speech.
3. Pure religion is demonstrated by holy living and deeds of mercy.

Lesson 3: Showing Mercy

1. Christians must not show favoritism based on external appearances.
2. Jesus calls us not to judge wrongly, but to judge rightly.
3. We are to show mercy to others because God shows it to us.

Lesson 4: Doing Good Works

1. Faith that does not produce good works is dead.
2. Good intentions to help the poor are made complete by taking action.
3. Saving faith involves our whole being: head, heart, and hands.

Lesson 5: Guiding with Godly Speech

1.   Serving the Lord involves taming the tongue to bless people.
2.   Church leaders have a responsibility to guide wisely with their words.
3.   Our words should reveal undivided loyalty to God and Jesus Christ.

Lesson 6: Seeking God's Wisdom for Holy Living

1.   We are to allow God's wisdom to guide our thoughts and actions.
2.   God is the one who gives us the grace needed to resist worldliness.
3.   Love for God and one another is the basis for holy living.

Lesson 7: Relying on God in Humility

1.   Remember that your future plans are subject to God's sovereign will.
2.   Avoid the sins of the arrogant rich: self-reliance, hoarding, defrauding, complacent self-indulgence, and oppression of the poor.
3.   Wait patiently for God's justice until Christ returns.

Lesson 8: Praying for One Another

1.   We should pray in all kinds of circumstances.
2.   We are to pray for each other's burdens in accordance with God's will.
3.   Christians have a responsibility to care for one another's souls.

❧ *Appendix B* ❧
Leader's Guide

This leader's guide is intended to help you get the most out of your group study of *Serving the Lord: The Book of James.* Whether one person leads all the lessons or the leadership is passed around, it is hoped that this guide will encourage and equip the leader to present the lessons in a way that meets the needs of individuals and the group as a whole.

The Goal of Bible Study
The overall goal of Bible study is for lives to be transformed through the power of God's word applied by the Holy Spirit. Studying Scripture should change one's mind, heart and behavior for Christ. Encourage participants to engage their emotions and cognitive thinking as they study, and put the truths of Scripture into practice in their personal lives.

Overall Planning
There are 8 lessons in this study. Each lesson is designed to take about an hour for group discussion, plus you will want to provide additional time for announcements, prayer concerns, and fellowship. You should feel free to make adjustments to cover the material in a way that fits your group's particular schedule and interest.

Homework for Participants
Everyone will get more out of the Scripture and lessons if they answer the study questions ahead of time, including the first lesson. Encourage participants to set aside time to do the homework. Thoughtful preparation will allow participants to follow the group discussion better, and they will be more ready for deeper levels of insight.

The reality, of course, is that most people are pressed for time. Not everyone will be able to fully prepare ahead of time. By all means be gracious to them. They will be blessed by participating in the group even if it is the first time they have read the material.

Leader Preparation

The leader should do the same homework as the participants. In addition, there are a couple of things the leader will want to do to be better prepared:

1. Pray for participants by name during the week. Lift up their individual concerns to the Lord and pray that each person will find time to study.
2. Glance at the Endnotes to see if there is additional background information for the lesson that will be helpful.

Appreciating Differences

A good leader will remember that people approach a Bible study text with different expectations influenced by their style of learning:[43]

- Imaginative learners want to see the big picture and know why the information is important before they get started.
- Analytic learners like lots of facts and details and enjoy learning information for its own sake.
- Common sense learners solve problems and want to put the information to practical use.
- Dynamic learners are creative and want to find ways to apply the information in their personal life.

Keep in mind that people also have different learning modes. Your preferred mode may or may not match others in the group. For instance, visual learners tend to like maps and auditory learners may appreciate poetry.

People take part in Bible study groups for a number of valid reasons. Some people hunger to know God's word more deeply or need a safe place to ask hard spiritual questions, while others long for comforting fellowship and intercessory prayer. Some may just be curious.

Ask the Lord to help you be compassionate and sensitive to the wide range of learning styles, modes, motivations, and needs among your group.

Leading the Lesson

Start with a prayer asking the Holy Spirit to enlighten your hearts and minds with the truth of Scripture and apply it to your lives.

Part I: Setting the Stage

Read the opening pages out loud. These remarks tell what the lesson is about, why it is important, and relevant background material. Imaginative learners will benefit from knowing the big picture of the lesson up front.

Part II: Studying Scripture

Ask a volunteer to read the Scripture passage out loud. Do not press someone to read in front of others if they are not comfortable. Be kind and supportive if someone gets a passage with names that are difficult to pronounce.

Read each study question out loud and invite answers. Most of your time will be spent on these questions. The leader should not be the first to answer the study questions and should not even add further comments if the group's answers are sufficient. Watch the time and try not to let anyone dominate the discussion. Analytic learners will especially enjoy this part of the lesson with its emphasis on facts and interpretation of Scripture.

Part III: Personal Application and Growth

Read each application point out loud and invite answers to the questions. If a point is too personal, allow people to reflect silently on their commitment to change. Ask if anyone wants to offer additional points of application.

Dynamic and common sense learners will welcome the chance to apply the lesson in practical ways in the coming week. All learning styles will benefit from questions that challenge them to envision the way their faith will mature as a result of applying the lesson.

Part IV: Closing Prayer

Read Andrew Murray's devotion out loud and close with a brief prayer of your own.

∽ *Appendix C* ∾
About Hermeneutics

"Then we will no longer be infants, tossed back and forth by the waves,
and blown here and there by every wind of teaching..."
(Ephesians 4:14)

Certain principles guide our study of the Bible so that we remain faithful
to the Biblical text. We do not want to get lost in unfounded speculation.
It is considered good procedure when police detectives follow established
guidelines during investigations so they do not overlook evidence or draw
wrong conclusions. Similarly, we will follow established guidelines for Bible
study. These guidelines belong to the field of hermeneutics (her-men-OO-ticks).

Everyone studies the Bible with a hermeneutic, a set of interpretive principles.
Even people who have never heard of the word can appreciate that the way
they interpret a passage is influenced by their understanding of history,
grammar, and logic. One thing that can make Bible study perplexing, though,
is that there is no definitive hermeneutic with which everyone agrees. That
means different scholars might come up with different interpretations of a
passage depending on which interpretive principles they apply.

The choice of interpretive principles is extremely important since a
faulty hermeneutic can lead even well-meaning people to misguided
conclusions. Evangelical scholars generally adhere to certain traditional
rules of interpretation based on Reformation principles covering four
areas: historical, cultural, theological, and literary. This is the grammatico-
historical approach. It is designed to discover the author's original intended
meaning by looking at the background, context, theology, and grammatical
features.

The following list gives a few of the principles this study is based on. A good study Bible like *The Reformation Study Bible (ESV)* can provide some of the background, language analysis, and commentary suggested below.

Seven Principles of Interpretation

1. Consider the historical setting.

Study the period of history in which the incident occurred or was recorded. Learn about the rulers of the day, natural disasters, and major events. For example, look at New Testament events in the context of the Roman Empire.

2. Study the cultural setting.

Learn about the customs, food, clothing, religion, geography, and economics of the time. Consider the national and racial backgrounds of the people involved.

3. Read the Scriptural context.

Read the immediate context consisting of the paragraph and chapter in which the verse is located. Then look at the broader context of the whole book, other books by the same author, and the entire Bible.

4. Appreciate the unity of the Old and New Testaments.

When reading a New Testament text, discover whether it alludes to the Old Testament and what its connection teaches us. When reading the Old Testament, ask what the passage teaches about God's redemptive purposes which are ultimately fulfilled in Jesus Christ.

5. Let Scripture interpret Scripture ("the analogy of faith").

Interpret a difficult passage in light of related, clear passages. Read the clear passages first and then read the difficult one in light of their meaning.

6. Read the Bible in a literary way (*sensus literalis*).

Identify the literary genre of the passage (poetry, narrative, letter, etc.) Look for metaphors and literary structure. Remember that poetry, prophecy, and apocalyptic are not meant to be read in a consistently literal way.

7. Go back to the original languages (*ad fontes,* "to the source").

Study a translation of the Bible rather than a paraphrased version. The Old Testament was written mostly in Hebrew and the New Testament in Greek.

❧ Select Bibliography ❧

Commentaries

Kistemaker, Simon J. *James, Epistles of John, Peter, and Jude.* New Testament Commentary. Grand Rapids, MI: Baker Academic, 1986.

McKnight, Scot. *The Letter of James.* The New International Commentary on the New Testament (NICNT). Grand Rapids, MI: Wm. B. Eerdmans Publishing Co., 2011.

Moo, Douglas J. *James.* Tyndale New Testament Commentaries. Downers Grove, IL: Inter-Varsity Press, 1985.

Stulac, George M. *James.* The IVP New Testament Commentary Series. Downers Grove, IL: IVP Academic, 1993.

Faith, Good Works, Trials, and Suffering

Carson, D. A. *How Long, O Lord? Reflections on Suffering and Evil.* Grand Rapids, MI: Baker Books, 1990.

Guthrie, Nancy. *The One Year Book of Hope.* Carol Stream, IL: Tyndale House Publishers, Inc., 2005.

Murray, Andrew. *Working for God!* 1901. Accessed at http://www.ccel.org/ccel/murray/working.i.html; Public Domain.

Murray, John. *Principles of Conduct: Aspects of Biblical Ethics.* Grand Rapids, MI: William B. Eerdmans Publishing Company, 1957.

Nabors, Randy. *Merciful: The Opportunity and Challenge of Discipling the Poor Out of Poverty.* North Charleston, SC: CreateSpace Independent Publishing Platform, 2015.

Sicks, Chris. *Tangible: Making God Known Through Deeds of Mercy and Words of Truth.* Colorado Springs, CO: NavPress, 2013.

Tada, Joni Eareckson. Radio program transcripts from the Joni and Friends International Disability Center. 2015. Joni and Friends, PO Box 3333, Agoura Hills, CA 91376. Accessed at http://www.joniandfriends.org/radio.

Wurmbrand, Richard. *In God's Underground.* ©The Voice of the Martyrs. Bartlesville, OK: Living Sacrifice Book Company, 2004.

Leading a Bible Study

Bennett, Dennis. "How We Teach and How They Learn." *Equip to Disciple.* Series of ten articles. Lawrenceville, GA: Presbyterian Church in America, 2009-2011. Accessed at http://www.pcacdm.org/?s=how+we+teach.

Nielson, Kathleen Buswell. *Bible Study: Following the Ways of the Word.* Phillipsburg, NJ: P & R Publishing Company, 2011.

Prayer

Pratt, Richard L., Jr. *Pray With Your Eyes Open.* Phillipsburg, NJ: Presbyterian and Reformed Publishing Company, 1987.

Sproul, R.C. *Does Prayer Change Things?* Orlando, FL: Reformation Trust, 2009.

Reference Books

Berkhof, Louis. *Systematic Theology.* Grand Rapids, MI: Wm. B. Eerdmans Publishing Co., 1941.

Frame, John M. *The Doctrine of God.* Phillipsburg, NJ: P & R Publishing, 2002.

Grudem, Wayne. *Systematic Theology: An Introduction to Biblical Doctrine.* Grand Rapids, MI: Zondervan, 1994.

❧ Endnotes ❧

Introduction

[1]   Hegesippus, as quoted by Eusebius, *Ecclesiastical History,* C. F. Cruse, Trans. (Peabody, MA: Hendrickson Publishers, 1998), 59-60. Hegesippus' history of the church in five volumes has not survived except in the form of a handful of excerpts quoted by Eusebius. For more information on Nazirite vows see Numbers 6:1-8.

[2]   Eusebius, *Ecclesiastical History,* 59. The apostolic Jerusalem church did not meet in a central place but consisted of various house churches.

Lesson 1: Persevering with Joy

[3]   PART I: Setting the Stage, "Author"

In order to be included in the New Testament canon, writings had to meet certain criteria such as apostolicity (written by an apostle or close associate); orthodoxy (agreement with apostolic teaching); antiquity (written during the apostolic period before the end of the first century); and usage (widely accepted in the early churches). Authorship was therefore an important aspect of whether a particular writing was to be considered authoritative.

Not everyone over the years has received the book of James with equal enthusiasm. The early eastern churches readily endorsed it as canon, but western churches took longer to accept it, partly due to uncertainty about authorship. In the 16th century, the Reformer Martin Luther raised theological questions about the apparent conflict between James and Paul with regard to justification by faith. He also famously called the book of James "an epistle of straw" compared to Paul's major writings and the weighty Gospel of John. Luther did not dismiss James as worthless, though, for in his own writings he cited over half the verses of James as authoritative.

[4]   PART II: Studying Scripture, Question 1a, "James the Lord's Brother"

Jesus and James are called brothers in Scripture. In the New Testament when the Greek word for brother (*adelphos*) is used for a blood relationship it consistently refers to a sibling, not a cousin or other relative. Douglas J. Moo,

James, Tyndale New Testament Commentaries (Downers Grove, IL: Inter-Varsity Press, 1985), 22.

5 PART II: Studying Scripture, Question 2a, "James the Lord's Servant"

The term servant especially brings to mind the Old Testament prophets Moses, Amos, Jeremiah, and Daniel. Scot McKnight, *The Letter of James,* The New International Commentary on the New Testament (NICNT) (Grand Rapids, MI: William B. Eerdmans Publishing Company, 2011), 39, 63.

6 George M. Stulac, *James,* The IVP New Testament Commentary Series (Downers Grove, IL: IVP Academic, 1993), 31-33.

7 Andrew Murray, *Working For God!,* 1901, adapted from Chapter XXVI, "Labouring More Abundantly;" http://www.ccel.org/ccel/murray/working.i.html; Public Domain.

Lesson 2: Obeying God's Word

8 PART I: Setting the Stage, "The Perfect Law"

God's moral law is binding on all people forever. Its various purposes include showing us our sin and God's righteousness, restraining evil, and teaching us what pleases God. John Calvin, *Institutes,* 2.7.6-12; http://www.ccel.org/ccel/calvin/institutes.iv.viii.html; Public Domain.

9 Chris Sicks, *Tangible: Making God Known Through Deeds of Mercy and Words of Truth* (Colorado Springs, CO: NavPress, 2013), 21-22.

10 Andrew Murray, *Working for God!,* adapted from Chapter XXVII, "A Doer That Worketh Shall Be Blessed in Doing."

Lesson 3: Showing Mercy

11 Randy Nabors, *Merciful: The Opportunity and Challenge of Discipling the Poor Out of Poverty* (North Charleston, SC: CreateSpace Independent Publishing Platform, 2015), Preface and xxix. Used by permission. Nabors is the Coordinator of MNA Urban and Mercy Ministries, a church planting ministry of Mission to North America, Presbyterian Church in America.

12 Andrew Murray, *Working for God!,* adapted from Chapter XXIII, "Careful to Maintain Good Works."

Lesson 4: Doing Good Works

13 PART I: Setting the Stage, "James and Paul in Harmony"

This study is written from a Reformed perspective that sees good works as the *result* of faith: Saving faith → justification/righteousness + good works. (The Arminian perspective is different, for it sees good works as a *basis* of justification: Saving faith + good works → justification/righteousness.)

14 Louis Berkhof, *Systematic Theology* (Grand Rapids, MI: Wm. B. Eerdmans Publishing Co., 1941), 503.

15   PART II: Studying Scripture, Question 1a, "The Unity of Faith and Works"

The belief that one can have saving faith that produces no good works is a false doctrine called antinomianism (meaning "against the law"). Rather, good works are the inevitable result of saving faith. A true believer's life will always give evidence of faith.

Devout Jews acknowledge the importance of serving God through good works. In the joyous synagogue celebration of the Feast of Booths (*Sukkot*), based on Leviticus 23:40, an *esrog* or *etrog* (an ancient type of citron fruit that combines good taste with good smell) symbolizes worshipers who study God's law and respond with good deeds. In the ceremony three other plants that either lack good taste, good smell, or both, represent people who neglect to study God's word, fail to do good works, or both.

16   PART II: Studying Scripture, Question 5, "An Illustration: Abraham"

Abraham (Abram) declared his faith and God counted him as righteous fifteen years before Isaac was born. According to Jewish tradition the binding of Isaac occurred when Isaac was thirty-seven years old, meaning Abraham was declared righteous by God fifty-two years before the binding of Isaac. (If we accept the report of 1st century Jewish historian Josephus who says the binding occurred when Isaac was twenty-five, it would mean God counted Abraham as righteous forty years earlier.)

17   PART II: Studying Scripture, Question 6: "An Illustration: Rahab"

Rahab married Salmon and they had a son Boaz who married Ruth. Boaz and Ruth had a son Obed whose son was Jesse, whose son was David.

18   Andrew Murray, *Working for God!*, adapted from Chapter IX, "Created in Christ Jesus for Good Works."

Lesson 5: Guiding with Godly Speech

19   Joni Eareckson Tada, "Complaints and Evangelism." Excerpted from the "Diamonds in the Dust" Radio Program broadcasted on 08/07/2015. ©Joni Eareckson Tada. Used by permission of Joni and Friends, PO Box 3333, Agoura Hills, CA 91376.

20   PART II: Studying Scripture, Question 3b, "Words That Guide"

The Jews were not known as a seafaring people, but they were familiar with large cargo ships on the Mediterranean Sea. They also used fishing vessels for commercial and personal purposes on the Sea of Galilee. A 1st century sailboat was discovered at the Sea of Galilee in 1986; it is twenty-seven feet in length, comparable to the size of a modern speedboat. http://en.wikipedia.org/wiki/Sea_of_Galilee_Boat.

21   PART II: Studying Scripture, Question 4e, "Words That Destroy"

James uses the Greek word for hell, *gehenna,* derived from the Valley of Hinnom outside Jerusalem. This valley had once been the site of idolatrous

Israelite child sacrifices to the Canaanite gods Molech and Baal (Jeremiah 19:3-6), and later it was used as a place to burn garbage. It came to symbolize the place where Satan resides and the place of punishment in the next life (Mark 9:47-48).

    A word used elsewhere as a synonym for *gehenna* is the Greek word *Hades* which translates the Hebrew word *Sheol,* meaning the shadowy place of the dead. In the New Testament *Hades* is an unpleasant place for the unrighteous dead (for example, see Jesus' parable of the rich man and Lazarus, Luke 16:23).

22   PART II: Studying Scripture, Question 6a, "Undivided Loyalty"

    When Scripture says humanity was created in the image of God, we must keep in mind that God is the uncreated Creator and humans are His creation, separate from Him. Humans are made in the image of God in the sense that humans are rational and moral beings, analogous to God's being a rational and moral Being, although God is transcendent in His being, power, and glory.

23   George M. Stulac, *James,* 128-9.

24   Andrew Murray, *Working for God!,* adapted from Chapter XXII, "Ready to Every Good Work."

Lesson 6: Seeking God's Wisdom for Holy Living

25   John Bunyan, *Pilgrim's Progress,* Part 1; www.ccel.org/ccel/bunyan/pilgrim.i.html; Public Domain.

26   Andrew Murray, *Working for God!,* adapted from Chapter XI, "Faith Working by Love," and Chapter XII, "Bearing Fruit in Every Good Work."

Lesson 7: Relying on God in Humility

27   Douglas J. Moo, *James,* 174.

28   PART II: Studying Scripture, Question 2a, "Punishment for the Unrepentant Rich"

    The New Testament speaks of hell as a place of conscious, ongoing misery. Its location is a mystery and may be in a dimension not yet known to us. The attributes of hell include separation from God and His people, the presence of Satan and his demons, black darkness, a lake of fire, burning sulfur, chaos, destruction, and eternal torment. The souls of the wicked go to hell upon death and there is no possibility of repentance, forgiveness, soul sleep, or annihilation after death. The wicked will eventually dwell bodily in hell when their bodies are reunited with their souls at the end times.

29   PART II: Studying Scripture, Question 2c, "Punishment for the Unrepentant Rich"

    Commentators advise that the parable of the rich man and Lazarus must not be interpreted too literally. For instance, although there is a permanent gulf between heaven and hell, the chasm is too huge for the wicked and righteous to converse back and forth or even see each other. The parable is rather meant to focus our attention on the kingdom of God and its stunning reversal of earthly values. God has sufficiently warned us about the dangers of wealth and we need to pay attention to His word.

30 PART II: Studying Scripture, Question 3a, "Evidence Convicting the Rich"

One form of wealth was expensive garments (II Kings 5:5, 22). Another form of wealth was precious metals. Corrosion or rust is the oxidation of metal due to interaction with oxygen in the environment. Although gold does not react with oxygen and therefore does not rust, it can develop a surface tarnish from contact with sulfur and other acids. James' reference to the corrosion of gold and silver should be taken as an idiom referring to the eventual deterioration of possessions in general.

31 PART II: Studying Scripture, Question 3b, "Evidence Convicting the Rich"

Like James, we live in the last days. The "last days" refers to the messianic age, the period between Jesus' first and second comings. Our focus should be on living in such a way that we are prepared to spend eternity with Jesus. A focus on accumulating excessive wealth keeps us from focusing on eternal things.

32 PART II: Studying Scripture, Question 4a, "The Patience of God's People"

An abundant harvest of crops in ancient Israel depended on sufficient rain at the right time. The wet season (October-April) was a time for planting and growing: the light early or autumn rains softened the ground for planting; the middle winter rains were heavy; and the light late or spring rains ensured that the crops finished well (Deuteronomy 11:13-14). The dry season (May-September) was harvest time: first grains, then grapes (wine), and finally olives (oil).

33 D. A. Carson, *How Long, O Lord? Reflections on Suffering and Evil* (Grand Rapids, MI: Baker Books, 1990), 176-7.

34 Andrew Murray, *Working for God!*, adapted from Chapter XVIII, "Rich in Good Works."

Lesson 8: Praying for One Another

35 Wayne Grudem, *Systematic Theology* (Grand Rapids, MI: Zondervan, 1994), 1068-9.

36 PART II: Studying Scripture, Question 1e, "Pray in All Circumstances"

The word James uses here for cheerful (*euthymeo*) is different from the word for blessed or happy (*makarios*) in the Beatitudes.

37 PART II: Studying Scripture, Question 1f, "Pray in All Circumstances"

There is ongoing debate among Christians as to whether hymns, psalms, and spiritual songs are synonyms or three different types of music (Ephesians

5:19; Colossians 3:16). Another debate centers on whether the psalms are the only permissible form of singing during worship. The Greek word for sing or sing praise (*psallo*) comes from the same root word as psalm. Old Testament psalms were originally meant to be sung and some of them contain written instructions to the musicians; the original tunes have been lost but a variety of modern versions have been composed.

[38] PART II: Studying Scripture, Question 2c, "Pray for One Another"

The word used here for anointing (*aleipsantes,* meaning to dab or smear) is different from the word for the ritual anointing (*chrio*) of a king. The type of oil in view is probably olive oil. Olive oil was commonly prescribed in ancient times for maladies as varied as toothache and paralysis, but for James its main function seems to be as a visual symbol of the elders' faith in God's healing power.

[39] PART II: Studying Scripture, Question 5b, "Reach Out in Grace"

James' decision at the Jerusalem Council prohibited Gentile Christians from four practices. Three of the prohibitions were also found in Jewish ceremonial law. Commentators maintain that James was not contradicting his stand against the need to observe ceremonial law. Rather, the prohibitions spoke against detestable practices that were part of idolatrous Gentile pagan worship, and James was commanding Gentile Christians to reject such pagan worship.

[40] George M. Stulac, *James,* 187.

[41] Clement of Rome, 1st century bishop, as quoted by Eusebius, *Ecclesiastical History,* 59.

[42] Andrew Murray, *Working for God!,* adapted from Chapter XXIX, "Praying and Working."

Appendix B: Leader's Guide

[43] Dennis Bennett, "How We Teach and How They Learn," *Equip to Disciple,* Series of ten articles (Lawrenceville, GA: Presbyterian Church in America, 2009-2011); http://www.pcacdm.org/?s=how+we+teach.

Printed in the United States
By Bookmasters